For the last eight years Barbara has been my "go to" money mentor. She has an uncanny ability to bridge metaphysical wisdom with good ole-fashioned financial sense. Her work is a potent brew for anyone who is looking to attain financial freedom on their own terms. *Rewire for Wealth* is a soulful journey, one that will inspire you to live the wealthy life you deserve and can now finally achieve with Barbara's help!

—RHA GODDESS, artist, activist, CEO of Move the Crowd, and author of *The Calling*

We all need a push to be our own advocates when it comes to money. Huson is here to make sure we not only get the message but make the changes we need to rewire and reframe our money mindset. Her ability to raise the bar on our expectations for ourselves is priceless.

—BOBBI REBELL, CFP, author of *How to Be a Financial Grownup*

Having Barbara Huson as my money coach has been transformative, and from my perspective she is the most profound teacher and healer of money relationships of our time. This is a critical book I encourage everyone to read because a more equitable and thriving future is not possible without financial wellbeing.

—CLAUDIA CHAN, creator of S.H.E. Summit and *New York Times* celebrated author of *This Is How We Rise*

Barbara's passion is helping women get smarter about money so they can confidently make the best financial decisions. Her story, which she shares in more detail than ever before, illustrates how the path from confusion to understanding can lead us to unexpected places.

—**LIZ WESTON,** CFP, personal finance columnist and
author of *Your Credit Score*

Barbara Houson holds the master keys to financial empowerment for smart, conscious women in our time. Through her brilliant, wise, and inspired writings, talks, and programs, she will show you the pathway to create lasting wealth as a gateway to something even more important: your brightest future. I can't recommend her work more highly.

—**CLAIRE ZAMMIT,** PhD, founder, FemininePower.com

Barbara Huson's book of gems offers the "how" of healing your relationship to money, not just by teaching you about personal finances, but by helping you heal whatever interferes with financial health psychologically, spiritually, and neurologically. Pure gold for the alchemists ready to energetically transform trauma-based scarcity into healing-based abundance.

—**LISSA RANKIN,** MD, *New York Times* bestselling author
of *Mind Over Medicine*

If mastering your money feels daunting, you need this book. Barbara expertly exposes what could be holding you back with simple, practical solutions to finally rewire your thinking and truly build a wealthy life.

—**DAVID BACH,** 10x *New York Times* bestselling author, including *Smart Women Finish Rich* and *The Latte Factor*

Rewire for Wealth is worth every woman's fierce attention. Barbara's long experience and savvy guidance can pay enormous dividends.

—**SALLY HELGESEN,** coauthor of *How Women Rise*

Barbara Huson is the unequivocal leader in helping women rewire themselves for wealth. This book will go down in history as a total game changer for us.

—**ALI BROWN,** Founder + CEO of The Trust

Every woman in America needs to read this book! Barbara Huson is THE expert on women, wealth, and power—and *Rewire for Wealth* is your guide to the financial freedom you deserve. This book will change your life, if you let it.

—**MARCI SHIMOFF,** #1 *New York Times* bestselling author of *Happy for No Reason* and *Chicken Soup for the Woman's Soul*

Barbara Huson has done it again. By digging into the ways women think about money differently than men do, she is able to chart a path toward lifelong security—and wealth.

—**JEAN CHATZKY,** CEO HerMoney.com

Barbara Huson has done it again—only this time, better than ever! She weaves personal stories with the most cutting-edge neuroscience to help each and every woman reach her greatest financial potential, with heart and humor. This book is a must-read for anyone who wants to enjoy the experience of wealth!

—**REGENA THOMASHAUER,** founder of Mama Gena's School of Womanly Arts and author of *New York Times* bestseller *Pussy: A Reclamation*

This book holds a critical missing piece for women when it comes to true financial empowerment. If you keep finding yourself stuck in the same financial rut, look no further. Your path to inner and outer wealth is right here in these pages.

—**KATE NORTHRUP,** bestselling author of *Do Less*

Rewire
for
Wealth

Rewire
for
Wealth

THREE STEPS ANY WOMAN CAN TAKE TO
PROGRAM HER BRAIN FOR **FINANCIAL SUCCESS**

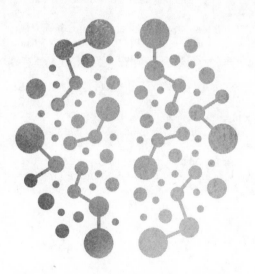

Barbara Huson

New York   Chicago   San Francisco   Athens   London   Madrid
Mexico City   Milan   New Delhi   Singapore   Sydney   Toronto

1 2 3 4 5 6 7 8 9   LCR   25 24 23 22 21 20

ISBN   978-1-260-46423-8
MHID   1-260-46423-7

e-ISBN   978-1-260-46424-5
e-MHID   1-260-46424-5

Library of Congress Cataloging-in-Publication Data

Names: Huson, Barbara, author.
Title: Rewire for wealth : three steps any woman can take to program her brain
    for financial success / Barbara Huson.
Description: New York City : McGraw Hill, 2020. | Includes bibliographical
    references and index.
Identifiers: LCCN 2020026885 (print) | LCCN 2020026886 (ebook) |
    ISBN 9781260464238 (hardback) | ISBN 9781260464245 (ebook)
Subjects: LCSH: Women—Finance, Personal. | Women—Psychology. |
    Spirituality.
Classification: LCC HG179 .H877 2020 (print) | LCC HG179 (ebook) |
    DDC 332.0240082—dc23
LC record available at https://lccn.loc.gov/2020026885
LC ebook record available at https://lccn.loc.gov/2020026886

McGraw Hill books are available at special quantity discounts to use as premiums and sales promotions or for use in corporate training programs. To contact a representative, please visit the Contact Us pages at www.mhprofessional.com.

For Jill Rogers

With profound gratitude for your

unceasing support, unconditional love,

and incredible wisdom throughout . . .

CONTENTS

ACKNOWLEDGMENTS

I'm forever grateful to...

My incredible agent, Michele Martin, for your astute feedback and your genuine belief in this project. If not for you, this book would never have seen the light of day.

My delightful and wise editor, Cheryl Segura, for whipping my writing into shape with your incisive editing and insightful feedback.

My wonderful friend Marci Shimoff, who in the depth of my confusion spent over an hour on the phone helping me clarify my direction and assuring me that, yes, I was perfectly capable of adding neuroscience to my repertoire.

My extraordinary coach, Ali Brown, for pushing me farther than I ever would've gone on my own.

My Spotter Sisters—Suzy Carroll, Kristen Manwaring, Teresa Verraes—for listening to my highs and lows and always cheering me on. This book is the direct result of your boundless encouragement.

My dream team—Lynda Jo Schussler, Carney Mick-Hager, Jennifer Clark, Jayme Johnson, Brandi Bernoskie—who, each in your own way, have been indispensable in bringing this book out into the world. And an extra special shout out to LJ and Carney, for your impressive skills and remarkable patience. I love you both.

My beloved clients, for trusting me to mentor you though the Rewiring process and in turn teaching me so much about how the process works.

My husband, Lee Huson, for your unconditional love and support not only while I was so deeply immersed in writing this book, but throughout our years together. I'll ever stop asking myself: How did I get so lucky?

INTRODUCTION

LIFTING THE FOG

What you do comes from what you think.
—*A COURSE IN MIRACLES*

I've heard it said that you can only go as far as your self-image will allow. Which explains why I spent most of my life in a heavy financial fog. Had I known then how to reprogram my distorted beliefs, I could have avoided years of struggle, frustration, and pain. I write this book hoping my experience, and the subsequent research I've done, enables you to confidently and joyously create wealth, well-being, and whatever else you desire and deserve. I can tell you, after being out of the fog for over 30 years, it's a seriously intoxicating high.

AND SO IT BEGINS . . .

The roots of our raising run deep.
—MERLE HAGGARD

I was groomed to be financially clueless. Not because of some malevolent plan my parents devised. But they, like their parents before them, and all preceding generations, were unconsciously conditioned by the prevailing norms.

Shortly after I graduated college, with a degree in art history, my dad took me to lunch in Kansas City, where I grew up. The city is famous for its fantastic barbeque. Over a heaping plate of ribs at his beloved Arthur Bryant's, my father came straight to the point.

"So, Barbara, what's next for you?" he asked.

"I'm going to apply to Berkeley, get a PhD in art history," I told him excitedly. "And then I'll become a college professor."

Teaching had always been in my blood. When I was little, my favorite game was playing school with my two younger sisters. And of course, I was always the teacher. Every summer, my family rented a house on the boardwalk in Atlantic City and I'd organize a day camp for the neighborhood kids. Naturally I was the head (and only) counselor.

However, my dad had other ideas for me. As he bit into a rib, he murmured, "That's nice," wiping the sauce from his mouth with a large paper napkin. "But you can do that anytime. Right now, at your age, it would be much smarter to get married and start having kids."

Despite my eagerness to go to grad school, I was unable to disagree with him. I worshipped my father. And it was, after all, the late 1960s. A woman's place was in the home unless she needed a paycheck. Even then her choices were severely limited. Growing up, I was not permitted to work, even to babysit like all my friends. The only job I was allowed to take (unpaid) was during my senior year in high school as a receptionist at H&R Block, serving coffee to waiting clients. My father, Richard Bloch, founded the business with his brother, Uncle Henry, so he had considerable pull. And I was overjoyed because the job allowed me to skip my afternoon classes.

I was never encouraged to go into the family business like my male cousins. And whenever I asked my dad about money, he always gave me the same advice. "Don't worry," he'd say, quite lovingly. He really didn't want "his girls" to fret over finances. In his mind, my sisters and I would always have a man and an inheritance to support us. Truthfully, I loved that advice. I didn't understand money, and thankfully, I didn't need to (or so I thought).

I came home from our lunch that day and still applied to Berkeley. But soon after they rejected me, by a twist of fate (or more likely, a wired neuropathway), I met my future husband on a family vacation. And indeed, a year after we married, I had a dark-haired baby girl, Melissa, who looked just like her handsome Israeli father.

But alas, motherhood failed to satisfy my yearning for . . . I had no idea what. All I knew was I wasn't happy. The solution seemed obvious. I tried to have another baby. But it didn't happen, and, according to the doctors, I would never give birth again.

I was devastated. Having children was what I was born to do, at least according to my parents. In hindsight, however, I'm convinced that my inability to conceive was my Soul's wisdom pointing me in the direction of my destiny.

I became severely depressed, though I doubt anyone knew. I hid it well. But I was hurting badly. One night, lying in bed, an idea dawned on me. Grad school would be the perfect distraction. Art history, however, no longer interested me. I got out of bed, found the local university's class catalog on my bookshelf, and started leafing through it. As the sun was rising the next day, I had decided to get a master's degree in counseling psychology from the University of Missouri in Kansas City. I honestly don't know why I chose that subject, but I suspect it was out of my own desire for personal healing. This time, I was accepted.

My depression began to lift. Life was looking up. While I was still in school, we adopted a beautiful baby girl, Julie, and I volunteered at the University's Women's Center until they promoted me to a salaried position. Though the pay was paltry, I was overjoyed. The rapidly growing women's lib movement gave me (along with countless other dissatisfied housewives) permission to enter the workforce and actually get paid. My parents weren't happy, but they grudgingly acquiesced. However, my dad told my husband he didn't want me talking about my job at family gatherings. That stung even as I obeyed.

I eventually opened my own business, The Career Management Center, helping what was then referred to as *reentry women* discover and pursue their passion. I vividly remember my embarrassment when my very first client left without paying. Asking for money felt horribly wrong and terribly uncomfortable. But I forced myself to speak up after that.

I was finally happy and fulfilled. Until the night, arriving home late from work, I walked in the door to find my mom, dad, and husband sitting silently in my living room, looking quite somber.

"Sit down, Barbara," my dad said ominously. "We need to talk."

I sat down tentatively. The tension was unbearable. I listened, in shock, as he told me that my husband had asked him for a loan to buy a house we'd fallen in love with. When my dad grew suspicious since I had a generous inheritance, my husband, a stockbroker, was forced to admit he'd lost much of it in the market, making wild bets on options, like puts and calls.

"Barbara, did you know your husband is *sick*?" my father screamed. "Did you know he's an addict, a gambler?"

I remained surprisingly composed in the face of his fury. "Yes, I know," I lied with aplomb. But inside, I felt humiliated, stunned, ashamed to admit I had no idea.

"If you can't get your husband to stop," my dad said, yelling so loud I was sure he'd wake up the kids, "I will take away your trust."

"What if *I* managed the trust?" I meekly replied.

We looked at each other incredulously. Both of us knew the idea was absurd.

After my parents left, my husband and I sat in quiet shock for quite a while.

"I promise, I'll never do it again," he weakly murmured the most familiar words spoken by every addict who ever lived.

From that day forward, my parents never mentioned my husband's addiction again. And even though I'd find out many times over the ensuing years that he was gambling (and losing), I still let him manage the money. That's how scared I was and how incompetent I felt. I kept hearing my father's voice telling me, in no uncertain terms, that making and managing money is a man's job. He was a product of his generation. And it seemed I was a product of my gender.

After 15 years, I finally filed for a separation. Not because of my husband's gambling but because he became physically abusive. I desperately wanted to stay married. I was petrified I couldn't make it on my own. My lawyer, however, handed me the divorce papers and insisted I sign them. I grudgingly agreed. Yet even after our divorce, I refused to deal with money. It wasn't my thing, I decided.

But as I would soon discover: *If you don't deal with your money, your money will deal with you.* Sure enough, I got tax bills for well over a million dollars, for illegal deals my ex had gotten us in behind my back. Of course, I didn't have anywhere close to a million dollars.

At this point, my ex had left the country, and my father wouldn't lend me the money. By then I also had three daughters (Anna, my miracle baby, was born right before our divorce). I was utterly and completely terrified. But I also knew I had no choice. Financial avoidance was no longer an option. I was not going to raise my girls on the street.

A SWITCH IS FLIPPED, BUT PROGRESS IS SLOW

We shall not cease from exploration
And the end of all our exploring
Will be to arrive where we started
And know the place for the very first time.
—T.S. ELIOT

I had no idea how I'd do it, but I was utterly committed, with every fiber of my being, to get smart about money. Little did I realize that my commitment to learn would flip on the rewiring switch in my brain. But significant progress would be excruciatingly slow in coming.

I tried reading financial books, going to classes, subscribing to newsletters. Nothing changed. I'd fog up and glaze over, proving to myself that my father was right. I felt hopeless, helpless, and completely alone. I no longer spoke to my parents, and my ex was out of the picture. I prayed desperately to God. "Help me get a grip on my finances. For my daughters' sake, if not for mine." God, however, didn't respond. I felt abandoned by Her, too.

One day, in the checkout line at the grocery store, I was mysteriously drawn to a conversation two people were having behind the person behind me. They were discussing *A Course in Miracles (ACIM)*. I learned it was a self-study spiritual text published and sold at a home a few blocks away from where we'd just moved in Tiburon, California. I bought a copy that day and hungrily began consuming every word, hoping to find solace within. The Course is a difficult read, and I struggled to understand it. Still, I sank into its pages like a lifeboat headed toward calmer seas. Where it took me, however, was actually quite disturbing (though ultimately liberating).

"Everything that seems to happen to me, I ask for and receive as I have asked," the Course told me.

Huh? That felt terribly harsh coming from the Divine. No way had I asked for tax bills I couldn't pay. Or a husband I couldn't trust. But the Course insisted, *"I am not a victim of the world I see."* Or put another way: *"I am doing this unto myself."*

I was aghast. How could this financial debacle possibly be my doing? Clearly, my husband was the bad guy here and I the ill-fated victim. Nonetheless, I was determined to change.

I made an appointment with a therapist. "Please help me get a grip on my finances," I begged him. "I really want to get smart."

What he said next seemed to come straight from the Course and went straight to my core.

"No you don't," he challenged me. "You really don't want to get smart about money."

I couldn't argue. I felt like all the air had been sucked out of my defenses. In that instant, I understood what the Course was trying to tell me. Yes, I chose this. That is, the part of me that absolutely did *not* want to take control of my money. The part that was scared of making mistakes and losing everything (better to let my husband do that!). The part that was nervous about my family's reaction to me changing. The part that held on to the belief that I was terminally stupid. But most of all, the part that was terrified that if I became financially savvy, a man wouldn't love me!

"No wonder you're afraid to get smart," he said. "Staying stupid has become an act of self-protection." Once I understood this, my avoidance began to make more sense.

I spent months getting acquainted with this part of me. The part that willingly gave all the power to my husband by refusing to participate in financial decisions, knowing full well he had a serious problem. I had indeed been doing it to myself.

Once I took responsibility for creating my upsetting past, I became highly motivated to protect my future. I hired a top-notch lawyer who claimed I was an innocent spouse. But my ex, a former attorney, wrote an impressive legal brief, explaining that my father cofounded H&R Block and I knew full well what was going on financially. I was devastated by his betrayal. Thankfully my lawyer managed to significantly reduce the amount I owed. I was able to pay the tax bills by selling everything left in my trust, except for a few properties that threw off a monthly income. If I lived frugally and saved prodigiously, my kids and I would be OK.

Now I had to figure out why the hell I stayed with a compulsive liar and gambler for 15 years, putting my family in danger, scared I'd do it again. I started attending Al-Anon, a 12-step program for those affected by an addict. It was there I found the answer, and it wasn't pretty. I realized I had my own "sickness." I was a raging codependent who was addicted to a raging addict.

I learned that codependency is a crippling condition in which a person completely disregards her own needs in favor of relationships that are often emotionally harmful and abusive. I had to chuckle when I read a *Psychology Today* article explaining that codependency is "when two people with dysfunctional personality traits become worse together." Yep, that was my marriage, all right!

I checked myself into The Meadows, a week-long codependent treatment program in Arizona. After successfully completing it, I spent the next several years religiously attending Codependents Anonymous and Debtors Anonymous meetings several times a week. Through this persistent work, I began healing the throbbing shame that had forever plagued me, but which I never understood.

Hungry for insight and healing, I signed up for personal growth workshops with increasing frequency. These workshops, combined with the personal and spiritual work I was doing, forced me to question my long-held beliefs, individuate from my family, and figure out my personal values and authentic truths.

And yet, every so often, I'd pick up a financial book or flip through *Money* magazine, still to no avail. The fog hadn't lifted. I had no idea, at that point, that I was already deeply immersed in the rewiring process, slowly reprogramming the false messages that had been embossed on my brain for over 40 years, in preparation for the miracle that was on its way.

MY NEW NORMAL

When I let go of what I am, I become what I might be.
—LAO TZU

Five years after my divorce, I was writing for the *San Francisco Business Times* when a local nonprofit hired me as a freelancer to interview women who were smart with money. Maybe God *hadn't* abandoned me after all.

During those interviews, women shared with me a series of surprisingly similar insights they'd each had, realizations that enabled them (and eventually me) to get smart about money. Those realizations turned into my first book, *Prince Charming Isn't Coming: How Women Get Smart About Money.* Spending time with these savvy women and incorporating their insights into my thinking changed my life forever. But the writing was agonizing. I was a working journalist and a syndicated columnist, yet I struggled for seven years to finish the proposal to submit to a publisher. Only later did I understand that it's not enough to know more or even think differently. I also had to consciously resist the astonishing intensity of old neuropathways while attempting to build new ones.

As I worked on the book, the fog seemed to lift. I not only got smart about money, but suddenly, unexpectedly, I was a financial expert with a whole new career. I began traveling the country speaking to women. In time, I forgave my father and my husband. In fact, I thanked them both. Because of them, I found my calling. But no matter how hard I worked, I couldn't make money, at least not very much.

That's when I met Karen McCall, a financial recovery counselor, who told me I was an underearner.

"I am not!" I protested. "I'm a writer." Everyone knows writers don't make money.

Then, on a cold January day, soon after crossing into the new millennium, I got a call from my agent, Candice Fuhrman. She sounded excited.

"I have a great idea for another book," she said quickly. "Women are now earning more than ever before. Why don't you interview these six-figure women and see what . . ."

She kept talking but I stopped listening. The thought of interviewing high earners—whom I imagined as designer-dressed snobs, totally intimidating if not downright boring and dreadful beings—sounded horrible. I hated the idea. And then it hit me.

"Hold on, Barbara," I said to myself. "If this is how you feel about successful women, how will you ever let yourself become one?"

In that instant, an unappealing idea morphed into a personal challenge. I ended up interviewing over 150 women who made $100,000 or more. (Among them were several writers—there went my excuse about writers not making money!) I not only learned the strategies that enabled these women to become financially successful, but for the first time in my life, I became a six-figure woman myself before I even finished writing the book, *Secrets of Six-Figure Women*.

By the time my next book, *Overcoming Underearning*, was published, I'd been making six figures consistently. So I set a new goal for myself—*make millions, help millions, and give millions*—which would be the subject of my third book. I began interviewing women making millions. Yet three years later, there was no book, no millions, and I was completely burned out.

My coach at the time said, "Barbara you're too into *doing*. You need time for just *being*."

I knew she was right. The next day, I made reservations at a nearby hotel for a four-day retreat. Holed up in my cozy room, overlooking water, I reread the transcripts of those interviews and discovered what I'd missed. I'd been so dazzled by these women's remarkable success and my desire to duplicate it that I failed to notice the most crucial piece. These women had succeeded in a very different way than the world models. I called this "other" way *Sacred Success—pursuing your soul's purpose, for your own bliss and the benefit of others, while being richly rewarded.*

In writing my next book, *Sacred Success: A Course in Financial Miracles*, I did something that petrified me. I came out of my spiritual closet, publicly admitting, for the first time, the key role *A Course in Miracles* had played in my financial growth. I wanted readers to understand, as I had, that wealth building is not just a practical process, but a spiritual practice, a healing journey, a Rite of Passage into our power as women.

After *Sacred Success* was published, I experienced a level of financial achievement I never believed possible (which typically occurs when you do what you fear). I honestly thought this was to be my last book, sure I had nothing new left to say.

SOMETHING WAS MISSING

There must be a better way to see this.
—A COURSE IN MIRACLES

It was after this that I had an experience that caught me off guard. I was suddenly, inexplicably struck by a nagging sense that something was missing. I had no idea what it meant, but the feeling intensified. I lost interest in my work. My passion disappeared. I was done. I awoke each morning, dreading the day ahead, seriously fantasizing about taking a sledgehammer to my business, smashing it to smithereens.

This was quite upsetting, shocking really. It made no sense. I loved what I did. Empowering women was more than a job. It was my mission, my ministry—it was why I was here. I didn't feel I was done working. I was just done with . . . something, but I didn't know what. I still loved counseling and teaching, especially about investing and wealth building. So why was I no longer excited? Could I be sabotaging my hard-won success?

I began praying for guidance. For months, I stewed in "I'm done/I can't be done" limbo. Eventually, I just let myself be there. Not trying to fix, change, or rush through it, but following the Course's instruction to *let it be what it is.* I canceled classes I'd scheduled, reduced my client load, and wiped much of my slate clean, eliminating distractions in my search for the mysterious missing piece, if there even was one. And I patiently (well, sort of) waited to see what, *if anything*, was next. It never ceases to amaze me how the Universe works when you finally surrender.

One morning, while casually checking my email, an article about *neuroscience* appeared in my inbox. As soon as I saw the word, I was intensely drawn to learn more. I imagine that some part of my brain lit up like a winning slot machine, hollering, *Congratulations! You just found the missing piece!* The more I read, the more fascinated I became.

My creative juices started flowing. My passion returned. Maybe I hadn't lost interest in my work, maybe it was just the way I was doing it. Maybe there was a better way to help women take the financial reins. I kept feverishly reading.

I learned that women's and men's brains process financial information differently. Men see investing in the market as a challenge. Women see investing as a threat. Since our prehistoric brains were wired for the sole purpose of survival, anytime we feel threatened, our rational brain shuts down, sending us into fight, flight, or freeze mode.

Consequently, women tend to avoid the markets in the same way our ancestors fled from wooly mammoths. We fog up in self-protection, become immobilized or hyper-anxious, and feel unable to absorb practical information, reluctant to invest, or we defer decisions to another, terrified of making mistakes.

This explained why I gave my husband all the power. My fear of loss was stronger than my desire to learn. But as it's often said: *what you fear, you'll recreate*. And that's exactly what I did. I was so terrified of losing money, I stuck my head in the sand, resulting in huge losses.

This also explains why, once women enter the market, they actually outperform men. Our lack of confidence works in our favor. Men, who are apt to be overly self-assured, tend to trade frequently. Women, with their lack of confidence, tend to buy and hold for the long term, which is proven to be a much better strategy over time.

The more I read, the clearer it became. Adding principles of neuroscience to my work with women would speed up their learning curve by cutting through their resistance. Instead of avoiding investing because it feels like a threat, what if they learned how to rewire their brains to become confident investors?

Over time, I blended three components that I'd long been working with—**psychology** (the study of the mind), **spirituality** (specifically, mind training as taught in *A Course in Miracles*), and **personal finance** (the fundamentals of wealth building)—with a fourth, **neuroscience** (the study of the brain).

Weaving together these four components, I spent a full year developing my own brand of what one neuropsychiatrist dubbed "self-directed neuroplasticity." This book that you now hold in your hands, *Rewire for Wealth*, gives you a simple three-step formula for altering the neuronal circuitry of your brain, enabling you to confidently and knowledgably create wealth and well-being.

In the fall of 2016, I introduced the *ReWIRE for Wealth* formula, for the first time, to a roomful of women at a four-day retreat in Chicago. Based on their enthusiastic response, I was eager to dive deeper into the material, working with women one-on-one and in small groups, taking them through the steps over a longer duration of time. I began offering *ReWIRE Mentorship Programs* and *ReWIRE VIP Intensives*, guiding hundreds of women through this process while I continued to refine it. I was astonished how quickly the steps expedited the learning process and how transformational they were. As one woman, Joyce, described her experience with the rewire formula: "My life changed so quickly that it was like going up in a rocket ship."

I will be introducing you to many women, like Joyce, who will share their stories, as I personally guide you through the rewire process. If you're like most graduates of my programs, once you understand how to train your mind to rewire your brain, you'll discover the immense power you have not only to take charge of your money but to change your life.

The motto for the University of Oregon (taken from Virgil's *Aeneid*) declares: *Mens agitat molem*. Or, "Minds move mountains." Those three words sum up the inherent power of *Rewire for Wealth*.

LAYING THE GROUNDWORK

"How does one become a butterfly?" she asks
pensively. "You must want to fly so much that you
are willing to give up being a caterpillar."
—TRINA PAULUS

Before you turn the page and dive into our first chapter, I invite you to do an exercise to prepare you for the journey ahead. I will be giving you a number of exercises throughout the book. I call these exercises *Rewire in Action*. They are meant to help you absorb what you're learning, enabling you to rewire as you read. I urge you not to skip these exercises. In this first exercise, I'm giving you a wonderful opportunity to flip the switch and set the rewiring gears in motion.

● Rewire in Action ●

WHAT DO I WANT?

"Our intention creates our reality."
—WAYNE DYER

This question—*What do I want?*—is what I call the Power Question. Having a firm, clear answer to that question—one that is based on your highest truths, not the "shoulds" that often guide us—is precisely how you claim your power. Yet, this is not a question many women ask. Nor is it an easy one to answer. But I'd like you to try. A strong, focused intention directs the frontal cortex of your brain to be on the lookout for strategies to achieve it.

In the space below, write down your intention for reading this book.

What new behaviors would you like to strengthen? _____

_____

_____

What unhelpful habits or patterns do you wish to change? _____

_____

_____

(continued)

What outcome do you deeply desire? _____

_____

_____

My intention for reading this book is: _____

_____

_____

Rewire
for
Wealth

PART I

Awakening

*All of us are born into a reality we blindly accept until
something awakens us and a new world opens up.*
—ASHWEETHA SHETTY, TED TALK

KICKING THE HABIT

If you don't control what you think,
you can't control what you do.
—NAPOLEON HILL

My intention for this book is to educate you financially, transform you personally, and harness the power of your mind to create the life of your dreams, make a difference in the world, and become the powerful woman you were born to be.

FOOLISH CHOICES

Until you're ready to look foolish, you'll never
have the possibility of being great.
—CHER

For decades, I watched myself make the same foolish financial choices, over and over. Maybe you've done the same, like . . .

. . . Avoiding money because it's so confusing and scary—*Why even bother?*

. . . Letting someone else, who's obviously smarter, make all the financial decisions

. . . Going on a spending spree instead of socking away savings

. . . Giving to others while depriving yourself, perhaps enabling them

If you can relate to any of these, I have two things to tell you:

1. You're Not Alone

When it comes to making long-term financial decisions and safeguarding our future, many women fall dangerously short. According to a recent Fidelity survey, over 80 percent of women, no matter how much they have or how smart they are, admitted they weren't protecting themselves financially.[1] For the whopping majority of us, money remains a source of stress, anxiety, and pain. If you're among them, let me assure you . . .

2. It's Not Your Fault

The truth is, you can't help it. Blame it on your brain. "Left to its own devices," explains neuropsychiatrist Jeffrey Schwartz, "the brain can direct you to act in less than optimal or beneficial behavior."[2] This refers to your finances as well as everything else. All the promises you made to yourself to be better with money, or all your efforts to educate yourself financially, won't change anything until you learn how to *consciously* create new neural pathways that produce wealth-building behaviors.

LET ME EXPLAIN

Habit, if not resisted, soon becomes necessity.
—ST. AUGUSTINE

Jacob Astor, the wealthy industrialist, once said: "Wealth is largely the result of habit." His words perfectly capture the central message of *Rewire for Wealth*: Change your Habits, Transform Your Finances. Sounds simple, right?

Here's where your brain comes into play. Couched snugly in your skull, this approximately three-pound organ the size of a large grapefruit controls virtually everything you do—inhaling, exhaling, spending, saving, and so much more. Every time you think a thought or feel an emotion, your brain responds with electrical/chemical impulses, transferring the thought to the appropriate brain cells, called neurons. These cells connect to either form a new neuropathway or deepen an existing one.

The more you think a thought or feel an emotion, like "there's never enough money," the stronger that neuropathway grows. It's called Hebb's law: *Neurons that fire together, wire together.* As you continue to worry about "not having enough," that neuropathway continues to deepen into a well-traveled rut until it becomes a hardwired habit. At this point, you'll unconsciously engage in behaviors that create "not enough," such as spending more than you earn, earning less than your potential or forgetting to open a retirement account.

"Whenever you repeatedly do something pleasurable or avoid some kind of overtly painful sensation," says Dr. Schwartz in his book *You Are Not Your Brain*, "your brain 'learns' that these actions are a priority and generates thoughts, impulses, urges, and desires to make sure you keep doing them again and again. It does not care that the action ultimately is bad for you."

If you want to know how your brain is wired, look at your life. But changing unwanted behaviors is far more arduous and complex than simply promising yourself, *Today I'm going to stop worrying about money*, and then consistently following through. Your brain, which is basically lazy and loathes change, will always take the path of least resistance. Every time you try to oppose an ingrained, automatic response, your brain cries out, *Stop! Don't do it. Danger! Danger!* And, despite your best efforts, you'll be sucked back into the hardwired pathway faster than a speck of dust in front of a giant Hoover.

But I have good news. There's another way, a far better way, not only to resist these deeply rooted habits, but to start forming new ones. This other way, however, requires that you intentionally and repeatedly defy dominant neural circuits. Think about it like this. In any situation, you have a choice in how you respond. Either . . .

- *Repeat* old, habitual behaviors with the same frustrating results
  or
- *Rewire* to build healthier habits with far better outcomes

Rewire for Wealth presents a radically different and proven three-step formula, known as The Rewire Response, for countering the intense undertow of entrenched neuropathways while constructing and strengthening new ones, until wealth building and well-being becomes your new norm.

WHY DOES WEALTH EVEN MATTER?

In a society that measures power in dollars, if we want to help women rise, we need to help women generate wealth.
—FORBES

For some of you, the mere mention of the "W" word may cause you to bristle like an irritated cat. Perhaps you're struggling with what the *New York Times* called the "moral stigma of wealth," thinking to yourself: "How can I be rich when so many are poor?" For some, amassing riches feels wrong, bad, sacrilegious, or just plain selfish. But consider the words attributed to Abraham Lincoln: "If you want to help a poor person, do not be one."

Rewire for Wealth is about far more than money. It's about the powerful woman you must become in order to create, grow, and sustain wealth. I assure you, it's the process, not the money, that empowers.

Too many of us have been in a deep sleep regarding our true nature, how powerful we actually are, or how affluent we could be. It's time to wake up. This crazy world needs awakened women (and enlightened men) so that we may go out and help awaken others. *Rewire for Wealth* is about awakening to the truth of who you are and the enormous power you have not only to create wealth but to generate change.

As the Rev. Michael Beckwith put it: "You can't be the light of the world if you can't pay your light bill." My goal in writing this book is not just to help you pay your bills but to empower you to shine your light at maximum wattage without the distraction of insufficient funds or disabling thought patterns.

No more dimming yourself down to please others or refraining from rocking the boat so you don't make waves. I *want* you to make waves. Big ones. I want to see a tsunami of awakened women shaking up the world, shining their light, and eradicating the darkness that's so pervasive on this planet. I want you to have the resources to do what you're here to do, wielding significant influence in areas you feel passionate about.

I truly believe when enough women understand how to rewire their brains, build their wealth, and claim their power, a global transformation will occur. We have the values, the vision, the sensitivity, and the resources needed to heal this planet. This I believe is our essential legacy, our inherent destiny, our utmost responsibility as women.

Besides, I believe money is our birthright as women. In fact, the English word *money* derives from the Roman goddess Juno Moneta. In ancient Rome, she was the guardian of finances. It was in her temple that the earliest coins were minted. And it was her temple that became the first treasury.

Beyond that, the root word for wealth, *weal*, means well-being. Numerous studies have proven the connection between money and well-being, linking lower incomes with an increase of chronic disease and shorter life expectancy. As I see it, attaining well-being is the ultimate purpose for creating wealth.

YES . . . BUT . . .

You must gain control over your money,
or the lack of it will forever control you.
—DAVE RAMSEY

At this point you may be thinking, "But achieving wealth feels like a stretch too far from where I am now." I completely understand why you feel this way. According to Pew Research Institute, the wealth gap—what presidential candidate Bernie Sanders called "a grotesque level of income and wealth inequality"—is the worst it's ever been in our history.

The disparity between the "haves" and "have-nots" has become a deeply divisive global issue. People are angry, frustrated, discouraged, and feeling oppressed by forces beyond their control, and especially vulnerable to hard times and unexpected emergencies. As I write, we are in the midst of an especially difficult and unexpected global pandemic caused by the coronavirus. Fear and uncertainty are playing havoc on the economy. Millions of people are out of work, who knows for how long. Practically everyone is feeling the pinch, though it seems the have-nots are hardest hit.

And women's finances are bound to take an especially brutal beating because the wealth gap is far worse for them. According to a 2018 JPMorgan Chase study, women own only 32 cents for every dollar owned by their male counterparts, *regardless of earnings*.[3] And as a 2017 Merrill Lynch/Bank of America study revealed, that can mean women will retire with $1,055,000 less than their male counterparts. The numbers are significantly lower for African Americans, Latinos, and millennials.[4]

Nobody knows exactly why the wealth gap is so widespread, though there's been all sorts of speculation: the

9

economy, foreign competition, layoffs, social programs being slashed, and for women, the whopping wage gap.

Certainly, these are contributing factors. But what I find disheartening is that everyone is blaming something "out there." Solving these external problems will unlikely eliminate or significantly narrow the gaping discrepancy, particularly for you personally. Take the Great Recession of 2008 as an example. Everyone, the prosperous and impoverished alike, lost money. But as the economy slowly recovered, something curious occurred. The poor were getting poorer while the rich kept getting richer . . . regardless of what was going on in the world. Will that happen again as we recover from this 2020 recession? Who knows.

But historically, after every downturn, there are the *enduring affluent*, those who consistently increase their fortunes over long periods of time. The question is: What makes them different? This is an important question. I believe if we keep blaming outside factors for our personal difficulties, we'll remain hapless victims. I'm inclined to believe what Thomas Stanley wrote in his bestselling book *The Millionaire Next Door*: "Before you can become a millionaire, you must learn to think like one."[5]

Besides, closing the wage gap for women will never solve the gender wealth gap. Just because someone makes a lot of money doesn't mean they'll keep it. I know this from experience. And I'll tell you why: wealth doesn't come from what you earn (or marry or inherit). Wealth comes from what you do with what you have. *The real measure of wealth isn't what comes to you. It's what stays with you.* In other words, your net worth—the sum total of what you own minus the sum total of what you owe.

GREAT NEWS!

Wealthy people invest first and spend what's left,
and broke people spend first and invest what's left.
—ANONYMOUS

Here's what I want you to understand. You don't need a huge salary or a stingy lifestyle to accumulate a sizable net worth. *Given time to compound*—when interest is paid on the accrued interest as well as the principal—*small amounts consistently saved and wisely invested can reap enormous rewards.*

I remember reading about a librarian who made $8,500 a year and left a $2.2 million estate. And another article about a 94-year-old bookkeeper who earned even less and was worth over $8 million at her death. According to the articles, both these women derived their wealth from *carefully investing their earnings.*

Putting money in assets (like stocks, bonds, and real estate) that grow faster than inflation is what creates wealth, but, of course, those assets also pose risks.

Unfortunately, too many women lack the confidence to invest. A 2015 Fidelity Money FIT Women survey shows that most women (71 percent) keep all their money in cash, which seems safe, but over time, our purchasing power will shrink like a wool sweater in a hot dryer.[6] After all, avoiding risk, which is precisely how our ancestors survived perilous conditions, gives us the illusion that we're safe from steep losses. The operative word here is *illusion.*

The fact is, the biggest financial risk you and I take, as women, is *not* that the market will go down, because it will. Guaranteed. And it will also go up. Also guaranteed. That's what markets do. They go up-down-up-down. But given time, the trajectory is always up. Your biggest risk, without question, is that you could outlive your money, regardless of how much you earn, inherit, or marry.

Case in point: I once interviewed a high-level executive in her fifties whose salary was close to $700,000 a year.

"I feel one step away from a refrigerator carton on the street," she told me.

"How is that possible?" I gasped.

"My biggest investment were shoes at Neiman Marcus," she responded with a heavy sigh.

Sadly, she is not the exception. In fact, there is little correlation between a sizable income and a substantial net worth.

Here's what's baffling. The Fidelity survey revealed that only 28 percent of women felt knowledgeable about investing—even though a whopping 90 percent of those same women truly wanted to learn. I find this quite curious considering the plethora of financial books and other edifying resources, like magazines, seminars, websites, and podcasts, that are readily available. The problem, as I see it, is rooted in traditional financial education.

THE CONVENTIONAL WAYS JUST DON'T WORK

The future is here. It's just not evenly distributed yet.
—WILLIAM GIBSON

For many women, investing is about far more than learning the mechanics of money or putting together a diversified portfolio. It's about who we have to become, and the amount of rewiring required to overcome a lifetime of personal and cultural conditioning to finally take the financial reins.

This can be a very emotional experience. But in an industry dominated by men, most financial educators take a strictly intellectual approach, deliberately steering clear of or barely skimming the "softer side" of investing or what's been derisively mocked as "touchy-feely" finances—in other words, shunning the very components that speak to, inspire, and motivate women. Beyond that, the emerging field of *neurofinance* (which combines traditional finance with neuroscience) has proven that most investors, regardless of gender, tend to act on emotions, not rational thinking, when making financial decisions.

Yet, pick up any money book. Chances are it focuses exclusively on filling our heads with facts rather than fostering our courage to change or bolstering our confidence to act. When's the last time you read a financial article about overcoming internal resistance from neuropathways programmed with false or limiting beliefs?

WIRING FOR WEALTH BUILDING

The real fundamental changes in our society have come about, not from dictates of government and results of battles, but through vast numbers of people changing their minds.
—WILLIS HARMON

I once read a quote—"We're drowning in information, but starving for wisdom"—that, to me, correctly describes the problem with conventional financial education today.

In *Rewire for Wealth* I want to share with you the hard-won wisdom I've gained professionally as an author, financial therapist, and wealth coach, from the extensive research I've conducted regarding women and money, and personally, from the 30-plus years I've been actively investing. Despite living through at least nine crashes, not just corrections (when the market falls 10 percent) but full-on crashes (when the market plunges 20 percent or more), I'm proud to say, I've done quite well.

My success has far less to do with the knowledge I've accumulated and everything to do with how I've transformed my thinking. Having grown up in wealth, I'm convinced the "enduring affluent" think differently. And as a result, they make different choices. As I now understand, our choices are determined by our brain's wiring. So, if you want to start making different choices, you must begin by rewiring your brain. Given the state of current events, knowing how to rewire has never been more relevant.

Here's where it gets exciting. Rewiring need not take a long time. As Norman Doidge, an early pioneer in neuroscience research, declared in his book *The Brain That Changes Itself*, "Massive plastic reorganization can occur at unexpected speed."[7]

Psychotherapist Richard O'Connor agrees. "The brain begins to change almost immediately with practice," he writes in his book *Rewire: Change Your Brain to Break Bad Habits, Overcome Addictions, Conquer Self-Destructive Behavior.*[8]

In fact, explains Dr. Andrew Newberg, author of *How God Changes Your Brain: Breakthrough Findings from a Leading Neuroscientist*, "Neuronal changes can take place in literally a matter of hours."[9]

The speed of your success, however, rests entirely on your level of motivation to change and your commitment to follow the specific practices that will effectively and efficiently challenge your cognitive networks. Initially, it takes tremendous effort to repeatedly focus on a thought that may contradict an old belief firmly wired into your neurocircuitry. Your brain will tenaciously defend your entrenched beliefs, blinded to anything that opposes them.

Unless you keep fortifying the new pathways over a period of time, warns Dr. Joe Dispenza in *You Are the Placebo: Making Your Mind Matter*, "you'll lose those connections in three weeks."[10] I don't want that to happen to you.

This book is divided into three parts. In the first, "Awakening," you'll gain a deeper understanding of the four components that make up *Rewire for Wealth*:

1. **Neuroscience**—the study of the brain
2. **Psychology**—the study of the mind
3. **Spirituality**—mind training as taught in *A Course in Miracles*
4. **Personal finance**—the fundamentals of wealth building

In the second section, "Rewiring," you'll learn a simple three-step formula for consciously reprogramming your brain. The three steps, which I call The Rewire Response, are:

1. **Recognize**—start by observing your thoughts
2. **Reframe**—find a new way to perceive the situation
3. **Respond differently**—consciously, not habitually, react in ways that don't feel comfortable

By repeatedly practicing these three steps, the old brain circuits will become weaker as new ones grow stronger. But in the beginning, old pathways can (and will) easily be reactivated.

In the final section, *Hardwiring*, you'll acquire three Power Tools to strengthen and secure the initially fragile new responses. The Power Tools are:

1. **Resistance work**—how to take the path of *most* resistance
2. **Reparenting**—how to heal your inner child who's likely running the show
3. **Repetition**—how to keep repeating the new behaviors until a habit is formed

Throughout this book, I'll be planting the seeds for the rewiring process. Take what feels right. Leave what doesn't. I urge you to take notes. Write down anything that seems important, either on a sheet of paper or in the margins of this book. Writing accelerates the installation of new neuropathways. But above all, be willing to accept that much of what the world has taught you about who you are and what you're capable of accomplishing could be wrong, or at the very least, woefully inadequate.

2

BODY, MIND, AND SPIRIT

It is never too late to be what you might have been.
—GEORGE ELIOT

MIND VS BRAIN

I am affected only by my thoughts.
—*A COURSE IN MIRACLES*

When you're young, your brain is constantly rewiring as you continue to learn. But until recently, science believed the brain became permanently fixed by age 30. Now, neuroscientists agree that *neuroplasticity*, defined as the brain's ability to rewire itself, continues throughout your life.

Ask those same neuroscientists, however, to define the difference between the mind and the brain, and you'll hear lots of disagreement.

Some will tell you the mind and the brain are one and the same. Others contend the intangible mind resides in the physical organ called the brain. Still others argue that the mind, being impossible to measure or objectively study, doesn't exist at all.

The camp that I found most compelling are those who claim the brain—a tangible organ in your body—and the mind—a nonphysical source of thought and feelings—are two separate entities that operate in tandem.

I was first introduced to this school of thought by one of its earliest proponents, Dr. Jeffrey Schwartz, a neuropsychiatrist at UCLA School of Medicine. Dr. Schwartz is well known for his landmark study successfully treating patients with obsessive-compulsive disorder (OCD) without using drugs.

In his groundbreaking book *The Mind and the Brain*, he explains how "directed mental force" (which he later called "self-directed neuroplasticity") can "clearly and systematically" alter the faulty brain chemistry of those suffering from OCD.[1]

"OCD," Dr. Schwartz explained in his book, "is a neuropsychiatric disorder marked by distressing intrusive, unwanted thoughts (the obsessive part) that trigger intense urges to perform ritualistic behaviors (the compulsive part)."

After 25 years of research and clinical practice, he became convinced that "the nonphysical entity we call the mind has the power to change the brain."

I was gobsmacked when I read this. If OCD patients could learn how to resist their intense urges by changing their thoughts and replacing compulsive actions with new beneficial behaviors, imagine what those of us without obsessive-compulsive disorders can accomplish.

Initially, Schwartz was shunned by his peers. However, a growing cadre of experts are now enthusiastically embracing his position that "the mind is the software that activates the brain's hardware." Or as others put it: "The mind is the master. The brain is the servant."

One of those, neuropsychologist John Arden, wrote in his book, *Rewire Your Brain: Think Your Way to a Better Life*, "You cannot change how you think and feel without changing your brain."[2]

Another, psychologist Rick Hanson, founder of the Wellspring Institute for Neuroscience and Contemplative Wisdom, put it more succinctly in his excellent book *Buddha's Brain: The Practical Neuroscience of Happiness, Love, and Wisdom*: "What flows through the mind sculpts the brain."[3]

I resonated with this stance straightaway. It clarified why I, a rebellious teen and an ambitious adult, so easily caved in to my parents' admonitions, so readily turned a blind eye to money, and never said a word to anyone about my husband frittering away my inheritance. I'd been wired that way from a very young age.

FICTIONS THAT GUIDE US

The greatest sources of our suffering
are the lies we tell ourselves.
—ELVIN SEMRAD

I think back to my first memory of money. According to the esteemed psychologist Alfred Adler, founder of Individual Psychology, "Our earliest recollections become a guiding fiction by which the psyche orients itself." Of all the incomprehensible number of incidents from my past, the fact that I vividly remember one particular episode explains why financial avoidance became my "guiding fiction," the compass point by which I oriented my life. Picture this:

I'm about four years old, standing on a step stool in front of the sink, brushing my teeth, my mother beside me. Holding my toothbrush aside, I turn to her and ask a random question, as toddlers often do: "Mommy, how much money do you have?"

Without saying a word, she shoots me a look dripping with disapproval. Her eyes narrow, her lips tighten, her unspoken message is unmistakable: "Don't ever talk about money! It's bad, and you're bad if you do."

As psychologist John Bowlby, the father of childhood attachment theory, explained, "We determine who we are through the eyes of those we love." In that moment, sensing the threat of impending danger (Mom's anger), I knew one thing for sure: *It's not safe to talk about money. I'm a bad girl if I do.*

That decision sent my brain into high alert, releasing a cascade of chemicals and currents of electricity leaping over synapses, transferring that thought to brain cells (neurons), which linked together to form a new neuropathway.

From that moment on, every time I'd think that thought (even unconsciously)—*It's not safe to talk about money*—and reflexively act on it, I'd keep digging an ever-deepening cognitive ditch until ignorance and inertia around money turned into my automatic responses.

In her book *Train Your Mind, Change Your Brain*, science writer Sharon Begley compares this neuroplastic process to "traveling the same dirt road over and over leaves ruts that make it easier to stay in the track on subsequent trips."[4]

Indeed, financial avoidance became my default mode and my comfort zone. I'd robotically repeat the same bad choices believing these choices would keep me safe.

Unfortunately, what keeps us safe as children will suffocate us as adults. My secrecy and silence on the topic of money was, in truth, an act of self-sabotage with serious repercussions. But, then again, aren't all acts of self-sabotage merely misguided attempts at self-protection?

Rewire in Action

EARLIEST MONEY MEMORY

Close your eyes. Take a few deep breaths. Ask yourself: "What is my earliest memory of money?" If you prefer, go back even further and try your earliest memory of all. And see what comes to mind. You made a decision in that moment, a decision which became your guiding fiction. What was it? And how has it affected your life choices?

_____

_____

_____

THE EVOLUTION OF THE BRAIN

If life is a struggle, not making ends meet, living hand to mouth, then your reptilian brain is in the driver's seat.
—DAVID PERLMUTTER

Recalling that memory while studying neuroscience, my financial passivity made perfect sense. After all, the human brain originated for one purpose—self-preservation.

To our prehistoric ancestors, survival meant avoiding all the lethal dangers that could be lurking behind every bush. To a 4-year-old child, survival meant avoiding anything that could possibly trigger parental disapproval. Belonging to a tribe was as essential to our predecessors' safety as it was to me as a little girl.

The human brain has evolved, over millions of years, in essentially three layers . . .

1. The *reptilian brain*, tucked in the brainstem, is the oldest part, working entirely on instinct. It controls our basic automatic functions like breathing, eating, heart beating, as well the fight/ flight/freeze response.

2. Just above the reptilian brain lies the *limbic system*, which evolved a bit later, adding emotions and memory to instincts. This system interprets all stimuli as either good or bad, scary or safe.

3. The third part of the brain, the *cerebral cortex*, the largest and most recent part to develop, is the wrinkly surface you see in pictures. The cerebral cortex controls what's called "the executive functions" or rational thought, allowing us to think through options and use language to express emotions rather than acting on impulse.

All stimulus goes immediately to the limbic brain, eventually reaching the cerebral cortex, enabling us to respond to threat at lightning speed and resort to reason later.

Here's where it gets tricky. Our limbic system can't tell the past from the future, the real from the imagined. Whenever a situation is remotely similar to a stressful or frightening past event, our rational brain becomes incapacitated by a flood of stress hormones as we spiral into flight, fight, or freeze.

Attempting to confront my husband about finances was akin to my ancient forbearers facing a hungry lion. I either fled the room or stood frozen in fear.

WHY WILL POWER WON'T WORK

You cannot make your thoughts or urges disappear by willpower alone. If you try, you'll be disappointed.
—DR. JEFFREY SCHWARTZ

Thinking back on my situation with my ex, I remember how much I tried to push through my avoidance. "This is not rocket science." I'd chide myself. "Speak up, for God's sake!"

But every time I'd approach my husband, I'd lose my nerve. I didn't dare discuss my situation with my parents. And I was too ashamed to tell the psychoanalyst I saw twice a week, let alone the banker who managed my trust at that time.

Once, however, I found the courage to visit a financial psychologist after I heard her speak. I had this strong sense she could help me. Indeed, she was gentle, caring, and reassuring. I left her office feeling, for the very first time, hopeful, even excited about what was possible when it came to my finances. But the minute I touched the door handle of my car, I felt a distinct slap on my hand and a voice in my head sternly warn: *Bad girl. Do not go back.* I never saw her again.

The feeble pull of my fleeting desire to become financially literate and confront my husband didn't stand a chance against the mighty force of a deep-rooted neuropathway.

Fighting the fierce gravitational pull of an established neuronal connection is an uphill battle for everyone. For one thing, you're experiencing an actual withdrawal from the chemicals (neurotransmitters) that the old thoughts released in your brain. And despite your best efforts to think or act differently, when under stress, fatigue, or threat, you'll instinctively revert to the neuropathway that offers the least resistance, helplessly repeating the same dysfunctional behavior you've been futilely trying to change.

A fascinating study at the University of South Wales explains why willpower alone doesn't work. Students were shown an image, like an apple or a cloud, and told not to think about a red apple or a white cloud.[5]

As you'd expect, most couldn't get that picture out of their head, which is quite normal. But what about those who swore they'd successfully obliterated the image from their mind?

According to brain scans, "Even those people who are good at suppressing certain thoughts still harbor traces of the thought in [their brain's] cortex," noted Professor Joel Pearson of the University of South Wales.

The fact is, any implanted thought—whether it's a picture of an apple or words of warning, such as "Don't talk about money" or "Life's a struggle"—tends to linger longer than you realize, regardless of your efforts to resist.

"Using brute force to not think about something simply won't work," the study concluded, "because the thought is actually there in our brains." Of course, the more neutral the thought, the quicker it fades.

Clearly, willpower alone won't work. But mind training will. To understand how to train your mind, we turn to Spirituality, specifically *A Course in Miracles*.

THE MIND AS MASTER

Thought creates the world and then says, "I didn't do it."
—DAVID BOHM

A Course in Miracles calls itself *"a course in mind training,"* and declares its sole purpose is *"to restore awareness of the power of the mind."*

Having studied the Course for over 30 years, I was fascinated to hear Dr. Jeffrey Schwartz explain in his book *The Mind and the Brain* how he successfully treated OCD patients "by harnessing the transformational power of the mind to reshape the brain."[6]

As the Course asserts and Dr. Schwartz echoes: *"An untrained mind can accomplish nothing."*

The first step in mind training begins with understanding what the Course calls *"the most important concept that exists in the universe"*: the law of cause and effect. The Course (as well as neuroscience, quantum physics, and many spiritual teachings like Buddhism) explains this law very differently from the world's more generally accepted Newtonian explanation.

To the world, a cause is an external incident that produces an internal effect. Someone does this (cause) and you feel that (effect). But this view is very disempowering. Blaming something or someone else for "making" you unhappy turns you into a victim.

According to the Course, nothing "out there" has anything to do with you feeling happy or upset. Your thoughts are always the cause. If you want to change the effect (your experience)—more money, greater happiness, increased success, better relationships—you must first change the cause (your thoughts). Who you are, what you do, and the life you have comes from what you think.

Even Einstein agreed, "The world we have created is a product of our way of thinking." I suspect some of you may be rolling your eyes and thinking this is way too "woo-woo" or "out there." I understand. But before you dismiss this theory, let me show you what a game changer it can be. While writing this book, I had an opportunity to apply this law, and it dramatically shifted the whole experience, not just mine but my husband's too. (Just to let you know, in 2012 I married a really wonderful man named Lee.)

One evening, I was telling Lee about something important that had happened earlier that day. Lee listened attentively, until his cell phone beeped, signaling a text had come in. He grabbed the phone, read the text, wrote a response, turned back to me, and immediately changed the subject.

I got upset, hurt, and angry. *What am I? Chopped liver?* Just as I was about to lash out, I heard the Course reminding me of the Law of Cause and Effect: *"The world you see merely represents your thoughts. And it will change entirely as you elect to change your mind."*

As Lee continued talking, I asked myself, "Do I want to make him the bad guy, or do I want to calm down and figure out what's really going on in me emotionally?" Trying to control or change Lee would be useless. Because, in truth, he was not the cause of my reaction. I was.

Then I flashed back to another memory, the earliest one I can remember. I'm three years old, standing outside my house, looking up at my parents' bedroom window, awash in pain. They'd just brought my newborn sister home from the hospital. As I stood there alone, I knew for a "fact," *I'm not important.* That arbitrary decision grew into a staunch belief that's haunted me my whole life.

I realized Lee's reaction was igniting that ancient neuropathway. I knew, in that moment, I had a choice. Do I hang onto my old story like a heavy satchel filled with lies? Or do I change my thinking to create a new narrative and a new neuropathway? I chose the latter.

What if I interpreted Lee's switching the subject differently? What if he wasn't implying that I'm not important? What if he simply regarded his friend's text as *more interesting* than my story? A more interesting text is a world away from "I don't matter." In that moment, I was using the Rewire formula you'll learn in Part II. I turned what could've been a big blowout with Lee into a loving, intimate conversation.

THE MIRACLE OF MIND TRAINING

Human beings can alter their lives by
altering their attitudes of mind.
—WILLIAM JAMES

As you can see, mind training is about far more than positive thinking. It requires you to take away the cause of your feelings and experience from the world out there and put it back where it belongs, in your own mind. Or as the Course puts it: *"Seek not to change the world but change your mind about the world."*[7]

When you understand the law of cause and effect, you understand how much power you have to create the life you desire. And when you understand that the cause of your pain or misery is your own thoughts, you give yourself the power to change those thoughts, and therefore, the outcome.

The fact is, the law of cause and effect, like gravity, is working all the time whether you're aware of it or not. It's how you've created everything in your life thus far, good or bad.

Rewire in Action

DISSECTING A CHALLENGE

Challenges
First, list any challenges or problems that are causing you some degree of distress.

_____

_____

Biggest Challenge
Pick one, your biggest challenge or problem that's got you tied in knots:

_____

_____

Ask yourself: What thoughts would I have to have to cause this?

_____

_____

Do you see where you could change any thoughts to eliminate or solve the challenge?

_____

_____

ONE MIND. TWO VOICES.

*You have power over your mind—not outside
events. Realize this, and you will find strength.*
—MARCUS AURELIUS

Just as science explains our brain evolved in three parts—the reptilian brain, the limbic system, and the cerebral cortex—*A Course in Miracles* reveals our mind has two "thought systems" or two distinct voices—the voice of fear, *Ego*, and the voice of love, *Soul*. The two voices offer wildly conflicting advice.

Your Ego is the spokesperson for the primitive brain. Its only job is to keep you safe by instilling fear—a job it's been doing since the day you were born, when your survival depended on getting love, approval, and attention.

Your Soul, which gets its marching orders directly from the Divine, knows you're safe. Its sole purpose is to make sure you soar, and it will continually nudge you to do what you're here to do, even if what you're here to do is scary.

The Ego urges you to hide and craves the comfort of the familiar.

The Soul pushes you to shine, favoring the uncertainty of the unknown, where all success lies.

The Ego makes excuses.

The Soul takes action.

The Ego focuses on your flaws, constantly comparing yourself to others, insisting you're either better than or less than.

The Soul, filled with compassion for self and others, reminds you of your gifts.

Here's what you need to keep firmly in mind: *the Ego always speaks first and loudest.* Just like it did during that conversation I had with Lee: *What am I? Chopped liver?* The Soul, whose voice is much calmer and quieter, requires stillness to be heard. In that discussion, my Soul was gently reminding me that I was hurt and angry, not because of Lee's words, but my misinterpretation of them.

"You cannot follow two masters," the Course warns. *"There is no compromise between the two."*

The voice you repeatedly listen to will determine how your brain is wired. Rewiring for healthier habits is simply a matter of unplugging from your Ego and plugging into your Soul.

Rewire in Action

WHICH VOICE ARE YOU LISTENING TO?

At the end of the Introduction, you wrote down your intention for reading this book. Flip to page xxvii and look at it again. Write it here.

_____

_____

Now, close your eyes and ask your Ego what it thinks about your intention. Write down what your Ego says:

_____

_____

Close your eyes, take some deep breaths, and relax because your Soul, which is subtle but tenacious, needs you to be still to hear its hushed whispers, its muted wisdom, and its loving guidance.

Now, what does your Soul say about your intention?

Write the answer here: _____

_____

What did you discover from doing this exercise?

_____

_____

SHAME, PAIN, TRAUMA

*The only people who don't have insane relationships
with money are those who were willing to examine
their insane relationship with money.*

—GENEEN ROTH

We can't talk about women and money without mentioning shame. Shame is a highly toxic, excruciatingly painful belief that you are so awful, so flawed, so worthless, that you're completely unlovable. Shame is usually associated with some form of trauma, stemming from something as violent as physical beatings or as seemingly innocuous as my experience looking up at my parents' window. Trauma occurs when a deeply disturbing or stressful event overwhelms our ability to cope and integrate the emotional effects. Trauma literally changes our brain.

"Traumatic experiences do leave traces," wrote Dr. Bessel van der Kolk in his marvelous book *The Body Keeps the Score*. "Which helps us explain why traumatized individuals become hypervigilant to threat. And why traumatized people often keep repeating the same problems and have such trouble learning from experience."[8]

I'm convinced that unhealed trauma and repressed pain are the major reasons smart, capable women struggle financially. When shame is triggered, our Ego, like a barking guard dog warning of impending danger, sends our primitive brain into a full-on fear response.

"It's like our IQ drops 30 points," Bret Lyon, founder of The Center for Healing Shame, explained during a workshop I attended. "We can't think. We freeze. We feel stupid. We're at a loss for words."[9]

Of course, our instinctive reaction is to bury those feelings under a thick bundle of distractions. I call it the *Secret Shame of Successful Women*. And I see it all the time. Bright, sophisticated professionals, making ample incomes, who have little (if anything) in the bank to show for it.

The problem isn't lack of money. That's merely a symptom. The real problem is all the bottled-up emotions we have spent a lifetime avoiding. And what better way to keep from feeling pain than to unwittingly create financial turmoil by forgetting to pay bills, splurging on gifts, or maxing out credit cards, anything to distract ourselves from the insufferable sting of deep-seated shame. These behaviors are similar to how others numb themselves with constant busyness, overeating, or other addictions. Unfortunately, research has proven that submerging emotions actually intensifies anxiety.

"Not only is suppression ineffective at handling fear, but it's counterproductive," explains James Dillard, distinguished professor of communication arts and sciences at Penn State. "It creates a cycle of fear—and it's a vicious cycle."[10]

Or as Sigmund Freud graphically stated: "Unexpressed emotions will never die. They are buried alive and will come forth in uglier ways." Buried emotions lock us into habitual patterns.

Years ago, I had a client who had struggled her whole life with chronic debt. The day she paid it off completely, she was suddenly flooded with scenes of early abuse. Financial tension had conveniently masked those terrible memories. I assured her these memories were coming up to be healed and she didn't have to slip back into debt, as most people tend to do. I urged her to find a specialist in trauma therapy, which she did right away.

As she later told me: "Facing my pain has literally led to financial gain."

But here's what I've come to understand, after decades of working with thousands of women. Money shame is ubiquitous *regardless* of one's economic status. I got my first glimpse of this many years ago, during a conversation with a friend. We began sharing how, growing up, we both felt a lot of shame around our family's finances.

I, raised in wealth, hated feeling different from my friends, never knowing if they liked me for myself or for my rich parents. She, raised in poverty, loathed feeling inferior to her classmates, always suspecting they pitied or looked down on her.

Essentially, money itself (or lack of it) is never the true source of our shame. Money is simply a magnifier, amplifying the shame we already carry, the traumatic memories indelibly inked in our psyche.

The secret to financial security, for many, lies in transforming toxic shame (self-loathing) into healthy shame (self-compassion), which Dr. Lyon, of the Center for Healing Shame, describes as "Yeah, I'm a flawed human being like everyone else and I have strengths."

When I witness a client continually repeating self-sabotaging behaviors, despite her genuine desire to change, I often urge her to seek therapy. I know from personal experience that the neuropathways carved out of painful memories can become set in cement.

According to a growing number of psychologists and psychiatrists, talk therapy is not always the most effective approach for trauma. As trauma expert Dr. van der Kolk points out, "The rational brain is basically impotent to talk the emotional brain out of its own reality."[11]

I sometimes send clients who are weighed down by early trauma to an EMDR therapist. EMDR, which stands for eye movement desensitization and reprocessing, is a therapeutic approach developed specifically for trauma victims.

I first experienced EMDR in 2003 when I was desperately trying to save my unhappy second marriage. After only a few sessions, I realized the marriage wasn't worth saving.

I recently returned to EMDR while working on the proposal for this book. Writing has always been a torturous experience. My Ego screams bloody hell: "You're a horrible writer. No one will read this. You don't know what you're talking about." Forcing myself to keep at it—which for some crazy reason I'm compelled to do—becomes an agonizing battle. When my Ego started up again with this, my eighth book, I made an appointment with Laura Rose, the EMDR therapist to whom I refer clients.

She asked me to recall past memories that aroused similar feelings of crushing self-doubt.

During the third session, I saw my young self looking up at her parents' window, certain she was no longer important. Laura asked me to get in touch with how that child must have felt. I had tremendous empathy for that little girl. But a split second later, a thought hit me. *She was wrong! It wasn't true!* I saw everything so clearly. My rational brain knew, without any doubt, that my parents genuinely loved me, that I was and always will be important to them. I felt a rush of gratitude for finally realizing I'd been living a lie my whole life.

After that session, my Ego's voice noticeably quieted down, no longer sending me into fits of panic. For the first time I actually enjoyed the writing, start to finish. And I'm slowly discovering who I truly am now without being defined by an erroneous belief that I came to under my parents' window when I was three years old.

Of course, not everyone has the time, money, or interest in going to a professional therapist. There are a number of other methods for treating trauma and shame, such as mindfulness training, neurofeedback, and EFT (emotional freedom technique or tapping). There is a lot of information about these modalities available on the Internet, and they can often be done on your own.

THE GOAL OF MIND/BODY/ SPIRIT CONNECTION

If I have the belief I can do it, I shall surely acquire the capacity to do it, even if I may not have it at the beginning.
—MAHATMA GANDHI

Let's conclude this chapter by discussing *self-efficacy*. This is a word that's rarely used in a financial context, but it is, without question, essential for wealth and well-being.

Self-efficacy—a psychological concept developed by Stanford psychologist Albert Bandura—is the belief that I can do whatever I decide to do, trusting I'll succeed no matter what.

Researchers Adele Atkinson and Flore Anne Messy, reporting on an international study of financial literacy, beautifully describe the importance of self-efficacy: "An individual needs to have the motivation to seek out financial information, the ability to control emotions that can affect their decision-making, and assurance in their own decision-making and financial management capabilities."[12]

In other words, you may know that investing is necessary to build wealth and retire comfortably. You may even be quite knowledgeable about the subject, having attended a gazillion classes and read countless books. But if you don't believe you can invest wisely without screwing up irreparably, you likely won't even try. Or you'll stop at the first stumbling block. Or worse, you'll unconsciously make bad choices that reaffirm your limiting belief, just as I did for 40 years.

Strengthening the neuropathways for self-efficacy is the secret sauce for both financial success and personal well-being. It's the difference between knowing what to do and actually doing it, between being highly competent and feeling truly confident, between traditional financial education and The Rewire Response.

A 2013 study of 1,542 Australian women, reported in the *Journal of Economic Psychology*, found "Women with higher financial self-efficacy are more likely to hold investment and savings products, and less likely to hold debt-related products."[13]

The research discovered that financial self-efficacy, far more than financial literacy, is the most powerful predictor of financial well-being for women.

For years, studies have been telling us that women are far less confident in their ability to invest than men are. I'm convinced that enhancing self-efficacy is the missing link for leveling that playing field. Yet, how many classes have you attended, professional advisors have you visited, or books have your read that gave you the tools to shore up self-efficacy?

Unfortunately, traditional education tends to focus on facts and ignore the inner work. This is one of the things that inspired me to write this book. I want to teach you how to increase self-efficacy by training your mind to rewire your brain to confidently create wealth, well-being, and whatever else you want.

3

THE WEALTH CONNECTION

It is not because things are difficult that we do not dare.
It is because we do not dare that things are difficult.

—SENECA

Welcome to the fascinating world of personal finance. Though I imagine, for some of you, this world feels more foreboding than fascinating. I quite understand. In this chapter, I will do my best to quell your fears by demystifying, simplifying, and clarifying what may be unfamiliar, if not forbidden territory. We'll do this by delving into four questions.

1. **What is wealth?**
2. **How do I create wealth?**
3. **Why is building wealth so scary?**
4. **How can I best protect myself?**

As you read the following pages, I want you to notice when your mind begins to wander, when you start spacing out or fogging up. If this happens, take a moment to look at why you lost focus. Maybe you're tired and need a break. Or perhaps your Ego, from its perch in the primitive brain, is trying to restrict your entry into what it considers a high-risk zone.

Just notice and either take a break, resume reading, or journal about your reaction. Of course, it's perfectly normal to glaze over when you come across unfamiliar terms or perplexing jargon. But instead of getting overwhelmed and giving up, or ignoring it and moving on, I urge you to immediately look up the word or phrase online as a way to further educate yourself.

WHAT IS WEALTH?

Wealth is not [hers] that has it, but [hers] that enjoys it.
—BENJAMIN FRANKLIN

Before we begin, I want you to answer this question: *How much money do you need to be wealthy?* _____.
Write down the first number that comes to mind. Don't read any further until you have your number.

Of course, you may argue, there's more to wealth than amassing money. There's love, health, freedom, and friendship. All true. But for the purpose of this chapter, let's stick with a specific figure.

If you're like most, you chose an amount that's more than you have now. Maybe a lot more. But here's what I want you to understand. *Wealth is not an amount. It's a mindset.*

I've met women worth millions who are financially insecure. I know many who have far less and consider themselves bountiful. Wealth without well-being is *not* the aim of this book. Financial well-being means you're in control of your money, not at its mercy.

I propose a different definition of wealth, one that describes the desired mindset: *Wealth means you have more than enough . . . and you know it.* You not only have some disposable income, but a buffer against debt, a prudent reserve for unpredictable expenses, and a safety net that lets you sleep all night. And you're fully aware that you're in good shape. In other words, *wealth is that sweet spot where money is no longer a source of stress or distraction, but a powerful tool for crafting a secure and meaningful life.*

Like any tool, however, you must understand how to skillfully use it for maximum benefit with negligible risk. I think of my husband's chainsaw, which he expertly operates. In my hands, I shudder to think of the havoc I'd cause.

This chapter is meant to be an operator's guide to confidently, competently enjoying the incredible tool we call money.

HOW DO I CREATE WEALTH?

Never spend your money before you have it.
—THOMAS JEFFERSON

To create wealth, all you need do is follow four rules, *in this order*:

1. **Spend less.**
2. **Save more.**
3. **Invest wisely.**
4. **Give generously.**

Admittedly, adhering to the first three can be a formidable challenge. It's tempting to head straight to the fourth, which is much more fun. After all, giving releases those feel-good hormones, like dopamine, in the brain. But the rules must be followed in this sequence. Bypassing the first three not only jeopardizes your future security but diminishes the impact you can make with your money.

Rewire in Action

RATING YOUR RELATIONSHIP TO WEALTH

Rate your relationship to each rule on a 1–5 scale: 1 is terrible; 5 is terrific.

Spending: _____

Saving: _____

Investing: _____

Giving: _____

Then ask yourself the following questions, jotting down your answers.

If you could change one score to 5, what would it be? _____

What if raising that one score to 5 was part of your intention for reading this book? Rewrite your intention from the Introduction (page xxvii) to include raising that score:_____

_____

On a scale of 1–5, how motivated and how committed are you to change it? _____

Pay special attention to those you rated 4 or less as you read through this chapter. Ask yourself: What's preventing this category from being a 5? Your responses reveal where you need to concentrate (and where you'll likely fog up) as you read.

The first three rules are the *How-tos*. Consistently repeating these behaviors—spending less than you have, saving more than you need, and investing in assets that beat inflation—is precisely how you rewire for wealth. What you repeatedly focus your attention on is what gets wired in your brain. The fourth is the *Why*, the reason you'll stick with the other three rules, despite your resistance. Let's take a closer look at each rule.

Rule #1: Spend Less

> *Too many people spend money they haven't earned, to buy*
> *things they don't want, to impress people they don't like.*
> —WILL ROGERS

Obviously, if you spend more than you have, you'll never have *more than enough*. At best you'll be teetering on a tightrope of barely enough. At worst, you'll be caught in the chaos of overdue bills and creditors calling. Debt and well-being can never coexist.

But even if you've always been frugal, I invite you to look closely at your spending habits. The best way to do this is by tracking your expenses, writing down everything you spend. Believe me, this exercise is not just for those with limited means. The numbers tell a story about your life. You'll discover bad habits and blind spots, where you're putting your time and energy, what's missing in your life, and where you're not living your values.

● Rewire in Action ●

TRACKING YOUR SPENDING

Here's how it works. Buy a small notebook or find an empty check-book register that fits into your pocket or purse. Whenever you buy something—a yoga class, a subway ticket, a cup of coffee, or pair of shoes—whether you use cash, check, debit, or credit—jot down the item along with the cost. Try to do this at the point of purchase. Otherwise, as receipts pile up, you'll likely get overwhelmed and give up.

I want you to do this exercise by hand, not electronically, at least for the first few months. Using an app may be easier, but the physical act of writing keeps you mindful and con-nected to your money. Otherwise, it's easy to rationalize your behavior and ignore potential consequences.

I'm not asking you to change anything, either. You can if you wish, but in the beginning of this process I want you to simply note, without judgment, how much you spend and on what. This is meant to be a *consciousness-raising* exercise. And it's powerful!

After a few weeks of tracking, my client Betsy Furler was excited. "Writing down what I spend, seeing it, made me feel so in control!" she exclaimed. "It made me think before spending. I felt so powerful. Every decision is *my* decision."

Don't be surprised, however, if your brain rebels against tracking. I remember when my mentor, Karen McCall, a pioneer in financial recovery counseling, first gave me this assignment, I resisted it for months. I'd start and stop, forget to write stuff down, and angrily refuse to do it. But as Karen kept reminding me, "Tracking is a tool, not a weapon to beat yourself up." I say the same to you. Don't make yourself wrong if you fall off the wagon. Just get back on as soon as you can.

When I finally kept at it, I had some unexpected surprises. For example, I saw I was spending a fortune on face creams, and they weren't even working. Karen gently explained what I was doing here: "You're trying to fill a hole in your soul that no amount of money can ever fill," she said softly. I knew she was right. All the moisturizer on the planet wouldn't erase my deep sense of shame and unworthiness.

At the same time, Karen noticed how often I used a magnifying glass to read, even while wearing store-bought readers. When she asked why I didn't get prescription glasses, I heard myself say, "They're so damn expensive."

"Now that's deprivation," she said. "You're not giving yourself what you really need—good eyesight. But you're splurging on wrinkle removers." Then she said the words that deeply resonated: *"You can never get enough of what you don't really need."*

Tracking is *not* about sacrifice or deprivation. It's about consciously choosing to practice healthier behaviors. I remember Karen saying to me, "It's OK to have massages, but what if you had one a month instead of every week and deposited what you would've paid into your savings?" This advice applies to all kinds of things, from dining out to ordering online.

Tracking also stimulates the rewiring process by focusing your attention on healthier behaviors. In his book *The Power of Habit*, Charles Duhigg talks about a four-month study on willpower designed by two Australian researchers, Ken Cheng and Megan Oaten. After participants wrote down every purchase for four months, not only did their finances improve, but they smoked and drank less, ate less junk food, and were more productive.

"As people strengthened their willpower muscles [i.e., neuropathways] in one part of their lives [i.e., brain]," Duhigg wrote, "that strength spilled over into what they ate or how hard they worked. Once willpower became stronger, it touched everything."[1]

Eventually, you'll sort your expenses into various categories: mortgage, car, groceries, dining out, medical, and so on. Include categories you might be neglecting, like vacations, clothing, or personal care. For this, I suggest you use one of the many popular budgeting apps.

Once you see which items are fixed costs, you'll know where you can shave and save and, of course, pay down debt. I urge you to pay off your debt as quickly as possible. And stop using credit cards. Wealth is unsustainable while your bills go unpaid.

Rule #2: Save More

For every ten coins thou placest within thy
purse take out for use but nine.
—GEORGE SAMUEL CLASON

The first rule, spend less, sets you up for the second, save more by paying yourself first. Every time money comes in, put a portion into personal savings. How much? Ten percent is ideal, but less is absolutely fine.

Sadly, few people do this. A 2019 Federal Reserve report found that only two in five Americans could cover an unexpected $400 expense. Why do so many save so little? The fault may lie in our brains. The *Wall Street Journal* reported that Cornell University neuroscientists discovered that our brains are biased toward earning and against saving.[2] Perhaps it's the immediate gratification our paychecks offer, while putting aside small amounts feels about as gratifying as watching grass grow.

"Fundamentally it comes down to this: saving is less valuable to our brains, which devote less attentional resources to it," study coauthor Adam Anderson, associate professor of human development, told the *Journal*. "Our brains find saving more difficult to attend to."

Yet fixating on earnings can be foolhardy. I call it the *illusion of affluence*. I see it all the time. Successful women spending too much, saving too little, and plowing all profits back into their businesses or into classes for personal growth (deceptively calling it "an investment"). Their ample earnings give them the illusion, but not the security, of true abundance. As I've said before, wealth doesn't come from what you earn, but from what you do with what you earn (which we'll be covering next).

For many, setting aside savings is akin to self-imposed poverty, as expressed in a recent email I received from a fan: "How can I SAVE money to create wealth (which means cutting back spending) and still have a feeling of ABUNDANCE (which means the desire to SPEND) and not a mentality of LACK?"

In her mind, spending provided the pleasurable pretense of prosperity, while savings felt like self-denial. But a brain wired for wealth views it quite differently. Saving means you're giving the money to *you* (not Visa or Starbucks) so that ultimately you can purchase whatever you please without pressure or worry. The difference between the two mind-sets is not deprivation but delayed gratification. The ability to delay gratification is a sign of maturity and the quickest way to accumulate *more than enough*.

The best part: Saving is so easy when you automate. Simply contact your bank (online or in person), fill out a form instructing them to automatically transfer a certain amount (no matter how small) each month from your checking account to your savings account. You don't miss what you don't see. And, with little effort, you set the rewire process in motion. As you watch your savings swell, the reward centers of your brain light up, and your inclination to save more increases by the day.

But what if you can't come up with even a few spare dollars by month's end? I remember asking my client Dionne Thomas, who had zero savings, what she did with extra money.

"Extra money?" she gasped incredulously. "What's that?"

She, like most, frittered away more than she realized on frivolous items leaving little if anything left over. It actually never occurred to her she had a choice. No one in her family ever saved.

"I never understood extra money," she laughed when I interviewed her much later. "But once I started tracking my money and paying attention to it, I always put a portion of what I don't spend into the bank."

After making savings a priority, within a few months she had several hundred dollars sitting in a savings account. "Now at the end of every week, I'm able to pay my bills and still save. I've never been so excited about savings," she said, telling me how amazing it was that she had enough set aside to get an abscessed tooth fixed when she was in terrible pain and buy new tires when she needed them for a road trip.

Here's a simple way to start making savings a habit. Each night drop any loose change from your wallet into a jar, and every month, bank the savings. I once had a client who, on the day her grandson was born, quit smoking, putting the daily cost of the cigarettes directly into savings. By the time her grandson graduated from high school, she could pay his college tuition. Another began collecting coins she found in pockets doing laundry and cash from the coupons she redeemed at the market to make her first purchase of stock— three shares of Disney. Never underestimate the power of small amounts consistently saved.

Rewire in Action

SHAVE AND SAVE

Let's look at where can you shave and save. As you keep track of your spending, start noticing where you could possibly spend a little less and deposit that amount into a savings account. During our Rewire Mentorship Program, New Yorker Jazmine Roberts made an appointment for a massage, which her body desperately needed. When she found out it cost $180, she did some research and found a place in Chinatown that charged $39. She deposited the difference. She did the same with eating out, which she discovered she and her husband did almost every night. Now they dine out only once a week during weekends.

I recommend setting aside at least 8 to 12 months in living expenses. That may take some time, but it's a good goal to shoot for. I also recommend having two types of savings accounts: First, start an *untouchable account* for emergencies and unexpected expenses. And since a shoe sale isn't an emergency, open a *touchable account* for fun things like new shoes, a vacation, or movie nights. Having the latter keeps you from dipping into your emergency savings or feeling deprived.

Rule #3: Invest Wisely

> *How many millionaires do you know who have become wealthy by investing in savings accounts? I rest my case.*
> —ROBERT G. ALLEN

When you comply with the third rule—invest wisely by putting money into assets that grow faster than inflation—you move into the world of wealth creation. (Warning: In this section you may stumble on some confusing or unfamiliar terms. As I suggested earlier, look them up before you read further.)

Granted, investing can be daunting and easy to ignore, even for women who work in the financial industry. I can't tell you how many bankers, CFOs, financial advisors, mortgage brokers, and money coaches come up to me after a speech and say in total embarrassment, "I do this for a living, but my own finances are a wreck" or "I manage millions of dollars, but when it comes to my own checkbook, I feel like a klutz."

Just now as I write, I'm interrupted by an email from an investment advisor that says: "Even knowing the facts, I get stopped dead in my tracks, unable to manage my own money."

This makes perfect sense if you remember our discussion in the last chapter. Financial literacy doesn't predict financial efficacy. Knowledge has no power against a highly activated primitive brain.

Investing doesn't need to be complicated or intimidating, as long as you do the work of rewiring for wealth. Paraphrasing the legendary stock picker Peter Lynch, there's nothing about investing that a fifth grader couldn't understand. To which your Ego angrily retorts, "That's bulls**t!"

Let me show you how simple investing really is. There are only *two ways to invest*. You either *own* or *loan*. And there are only *five places to invest*, known as *asset classes*:

1. **Stocks.** You *own* shares in a company.
2. **Bonds.** You *loan* money to a company, state, city, or government.
3. **Real estate.** You *own* houses, buildings, or land.
4. **Cash or cash equivalents.** You *loan* money to the bank, a money market fund, a certificate of deposit (CD), or short-term Treasury bills.
5. **Commodities.** You *own* raw materials, like gold or oil, or agricultural products, like wheat or pork bellies.

Let's compare how each asset class has performed against inflation. After all, one reason you invest is to prevent your entire savings from being gobbled up by rising prices.

- Inflation has averaged 3.5 percent annually.
- Cash has averaged about 3 percent annually (though at this writing, returns are less than 2 percent).
- Stocks average just over 9 percent annually.
- Real estate averages about 6.2 percent annually.
- Bonds average about 5 percent annually.
- Commodities return 6.9 percent annually.

Can you see why at least a portion of your cash needs to be in assets that outpace inflation? According to the 2019 Ellevest Census, women who fail to invest leave anywhere from $50,000 to over $1 million on the table. Avoidance comes with a high price tag.

We can't talk about investing without mentioning the Rule of 72, a formula to determine how long your investment will take to double. The formula is simple: Divide the annual rate of return into 72. Let's say you own a fund that returns an average of 8 percent annually. If you divide 72 by 8, it will take 9 years to double your money. Put that same amount in the bank, paying 1 percent interest, and it'll take 72 years to double. Even if interest goes up to 3 percent, you'll need 24 years to double that cash.

(This formula applies to debt as well. Let's say you're paying 12 percent on your credit card. Divide 72 by 12, and you'll see that your debt will double in 6 years.)

Rule #4: Give Generously

Only those who have a real and lasting sense
of abundance can be charitable.
—A COURSE IN MIRACLES

Often, during a speech, I'll ask the audience: "How many of you are knowledgeable or somewhat knowledgeable about investing?" Very few hands go up.

"Why not?" I ask.

"I don't have time," most will say. "It's too confusing." Or "I don't know where to start."

"Interesting," I muse. Then I pose another question.

"What if a doctor told you that you have a serious condition that would dramatically affect your quality of life as you age? I bet, no matter how busy you are, or how complicated it feels, you'd find a way to research the best treatment and make sure you get it."

Heads nod in agreement.

"Well, if you're ignoring money, you're saying that quality of life is not a priority."

Indeed, rewiring for wealth can be tough without having a strong *why*, especially for women. Unlike men, once we're financially stable, we're rarely motivated by more money. What drives us is knowing we can use our money to improve the quality of life for ourselves and for others.

In a Simmons School of Management survey, more than 70 percent of women polled report they are driven not by "perks, position, or personal gain," but to help others, contribute to communities, and make the world a better place.

If you're struggling with the first three rules or find yourself in a financial rut, try this. Focus on what inspires you and stop dwelling on what scares you. It's called *selective attention*, a powerful technique for rewiring your brain, which we'll discuss again in Chapter 6. Instead of obsessing about everything that can go wrong, try turning your thoughts to what investing offers you. Think about how having more than enough allows you to give money to causes you feel passionate about, helping your kids, your parents, people you love. Think about the exhilarating sense of freedom, security, and self-confidence wealth brings.

That's what I finally did. I started thinking about the kind of a role model I wanted to be for my daughters instead of fixating on my fear of screwing up. When I made that deliberate shift, I had no choice. Financial avoidance was no longer an option. And if my experience is any indication, you'll be saying what I hear every woman say when she finally takes the financial reins: "*I feel so powerful.*" Because when you take control of your money, you take control of your life. In the 2019 Ellevest study, both sexes agree, "Money is key for feeling in charge of your life." And for women, taking control of their money is "the number one confidence booster."

Rewire in Action

FINDING MY MOTIVATION

Ask yourself these questions and jot down some ideas here:

Why am I reading this book? _____

_____

_____

Where in my life would I love to give more (to myself, to those I love, to causes I feel passionate about)? _____

_____

_____

WHY IS BUILDING WEALTH SO SCARY?

In investing, what is comfortable is rarely profitable.
—ROBERT ARNOTT

Investing is scary for one simple reason: it's risky. Neuroscience research proves that you and I hate to lose more than we love to win. After all, losing had deadly consequences for our ancient predecessors. To this day, when markets crash, the media will declare a "flight to safety," as hordes of investors rush into safer investment (like US Treasuries) faster than a pack of panicked Neanderthals fleeing a saber-toothed tiger. There's even a benchmark, The VIX, or Volatility Index, that actually gauges investor fear. The market is the fearmongering Ego's favorite playground.

But here's where we need to put risk in perspective. Cash in a bank or CD (certificate of deposit) is considered the safest investment of all. There's virtually no uncertainty. But even with a government guarantee of return, is cash *really* risk-free? No. Of course not. You have *inflation risk*. Over time, as prices climb, your purchasing power plummets.

On the other hand, buying stocks, or shares of a company, definitely carries more risk. Share prices, even in the best companies, are always going up and down and up and down. However, when we talk about risk in this way, we're referring to volatility, how much an asset fluctuates, known as *market risk*. And you need market risk to protect you from inflation risk.

Keep in mind: Price swings only matter when you sell. Everything else is just "noise," the sound of the market doing what markets are supposed to do, bounce around like a rowboat on the open seas.

In my early interviews with savvy women, I'd always ask each one: "How do you have the guts to put money in the market?" After all, that's how my first husband lost my money. Their responses radically shifted my thinking: "I know my investments will fluctuate. I accept that," one woman explained. "I am also confident that over the long term, I will do well."

That was my moment of revelation. Risk is not synonymous with loss. Risk is an opportunity for gain. *Understanding risk is what makes you wealthy.*

You want to know your most dangerous risk? It's not the market gyrations. It's your emotional reactions. Our brain registers risk even before we're conscious of it. Consequently we tend to make rash decisions that rarely end well, even if we know better.

So when markets take a tumble, our emotions, especially fear, take over. And we make very bad decisions. It also happens in reverse. When the market is on a big run, there's a tendency to take on too much risk and follow the herd, like so many did during the tech and real estate booms. Either way, it's easy to go along with the crowd and invest too aggressively during good times and too conservatively in bad times.

"The investor's chief problem—and his worst enemy—is likely to be himself," one of the greatest investment advisors of the twentieth century, Benjamin Graham, wrote in his timeless classic *The Intelligent Investor.* "In the end, how your investments behave is much less important than how you behave."[3]

Now, for the good news. I'm about to show you how you can significantly minimize risk, shield yourself from devastating losses, and successfully stack the odds in your favor.

HOW CAN I BEST PROTECT MYSELF?

Be okay with not knowing for sure what might come next, but know that whatever it is, you'll be okay.
—ANONYMOUS

The question we're really exploring in this section is: *How do I deactivate a triggered limbic system (my fear center) so I can invest with confidence and not overreact with excessive fear?* Yes, the market is scary. No, you can't eliminate risk. But you can calm your primitive brain by practicing these five proven strategies to manage risk and keep your emotions in check, regardless of the market's dips and dives.

Strategy #1: Educate

Now that I know better, I do better.
—MAYA ANGELOU

Warren Buffet once said: "Risk comes from not knowing what you're doing."[4] He got that right. Your best protection against loss is making decisions based on *knowledge, not fear, ignorance, or habit.* And no matter how knowledgeable you are, there's always more to learn. That's what makes investing fun.

If you're new to the subject, however, learning about investing can feel like navigating a minefield. Your ego will shriek: "Get me out of here! It's dangerous!" That's how I felt for years. Until I understood the four stages of the Learning Curve. To get smart about money, or anything else, you much travel through what educators call a Learning Curve (Figure 3.1). Let me explain.

FIGURE 3.1 **Learning Curve**

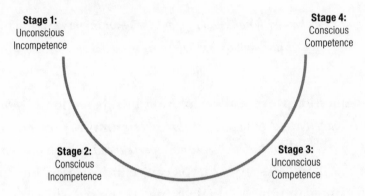

Stage 1:
Unconscious
Incompetence

Stage 4:
Conscious
Competence

Stage 2:
Conscious
Incompetence

Stage 3:
Unconscious
Competence

I lived most of my life in Stage 1 of the Learning Curve, *Unconscious Incompetence*. I didn't even know what I didn't know. The term "ignorance is bliss" explains why I never wanted to leave this stage. I fooled myself into feeling safe here, despite living with a ticking time bomb for a spouse.

It took a crisis—a huge tax bill I couldn't pay—to kick me into Stage 2, *Conscious Incompetence*. I had no choice now. I needed to get smart. Yet the moment I picked up a financial book, I was seized by anxiety. I couldn't understand a word I read. Everything in me yearned for the perceived comfort of the previous stage.

But I was committed. Big tax bills, three young daughters, and no money in the bank will do that. Despite my fear and confusion, I forced myself to keep reading, keep taking classes, and keep asking questions. Every once in a while, I'd get glimpses that I had moved into Stage 3 of the Learning Curve—*Unconscious Competence*. Someone mentioned the phrase "mutual fund" and, aha, I knew what it was. I actually read a whole page in the *Wall Street Journal* without once glazing over. But those moments were fleeting.

Finally, after months of flailing in the dark, I realized I was in Stage 4 of the Learning Curve, *conscious competence.* Yes, I still needed to keep learning, but I finally felt like I had a good grasp on the subject.

Staying on the Learning Curve can be extremely challenging. To keep myself going without holding back (at least not for long), I devised a simple two-step system I came to call *The Osmosis School of Learning.* I was amazed, in just a few months, how much smarter I felt. Small steps, consistently taken, lead to remarkable results.

- **Every day read something about money.** Even if it's just for a minute or two. Even if you only glance at the headlines of the business section of the newspaper, or leaf through *Money* magazine while in line at the grocery. So much of getting smart or smarter about money is familiarizing yourself with the jargon, the current trends.

  I remember, early on, subscribing to the *Wall Street Journal.* I'd lay it on the kitchen counter, and every day I'd walk by it, figuring that by osmosis I'd pick something up. To this day, if I do nothing else, I'll glance at the headlines. You can do the same with financial programs on TV or the radio. But beware the hype. Bad news sells. "The key to making money in stocks," declared Peter Lynch, "is not to get scared out of them."

- **Every week, have a conversation about money.** Preferably with someone who knows more than you. I learned so much from the women I interviewed, so whenever I met anyone who was financially savvy,

I'd pick their brain, asking them how they got smart, the mistakes they made, the best advice they were given, and for any other suggestions they might have. Generally, people were very generous with their time and knowledge.

I also attended classes. Podcasts are great too. But listening to financial experts made me wish I had a translator. *Financialese* is truly a foreign tongue. I finally realized I needed to speak up, ask for clarification, and keep asking until I understood.

Strategy #2: Plan

It takes as much energy to wish as it does to plan.
—ELEANOR ROOSEVELT

Not long ago, a woman in one of my groups proudly announced that she'd maxed out her 401(k) and had been buying stocks outside her retirement fund based on recommendations from a friend who worked at a brokerage firm.

She had a right to be proud. But when I asked if she was following a plan, she looked puzzled.

"How do you know whether or not your portfolio is properly diversified?" I asked her. "Or if you're taking too much or too little risk?"

Creating a personalized financial plan is what separates investing from gambling. Picking stocks or bonds haphazardly, following a hot tip or purchasing the hottest fund, trying to time the market (buying when it's high, freaking out and selling when it's falling), or just simply deferring investment decisions to another and turning your back—that's gambling, and it's genuinely risky in the worst possible sense.

Investing, on the other hand, is a means to an end. The whole point of investing is to put together a portfolio that ensures you meet your goals and protect your future, no matter what the market is doing.

The best way to measure your investing success," explained the illustrious investor Benjamin Graham in his book *The Intelligent Investor*, "is not by whether you're beating the market but by whether you've put in place a financial plan and a behavioral discipline that are likely to get you where you want to go."[5]

A good financial plan addresses three questions:

- **Where are you now?**
- **Where do you want to go (short term and long-term goals)?**
- **What do you need to do get from here to where you want to be?**

Armed with the answers, you're ready to create a game plan based on your time horizons, budgetary restrictions, and risk tolerance (your ability to stomach large swings in your portfolio).

For years, I worked with a series of financial advisors who put me in individual stocks. And I followed the guidance of my second husband, an expert on mutual funds. But I had no plan.

Then I met Eileen Michaels, a feisty, redheaded East Coast financial advisor who was whip smart and passionate about educating women. I instantly knew I wanted to work with her. Initially my intention was for her to manage only my individual stock portfolio. She wouldn't have it.

"You can't invest like that, without a strategic plan," she told me. "Keeping your investments fragmented is how you're keeping yourself small." She had me at "small."

"What is your criteria for investing?" she asked. I had no idea. So I gave it some thought and came up with a list.

First and foremost, I wanted to be extremely diversified because, by that time, I knew this was important. (We'll talk more about this in the following section.)

I also wasn't as concerned if my investments went up sky high in a bull market, but I wanted to be damn sure I was protected when the market tanked.

I was souring on the outrageous expenses of mutual funds, so I wanted everything in individual equities.

And I was very clear: I wanted to be involved in the decision making. That's how I'd learn.

Eileen then asked about my goals. How did I want to use my money? This was easy. I wanted a sizable cash savings, probably more than she'd advise, but after being married to a gambler, I needed a hefty cushion to feel safe. We talked about how my second husband and I were thinking of moving, so I'd probably need money for a house. We discussed my kid's education, my income as a writer, my fantasy of flying private someday.

Based on these conversations, she drew up a plan making sure I was taking enough risk to have growth, but not so much that I'd get spooked. Then she put that plan into action, creating a diversified portfolio of stocks and bonds.

There was one problem, however. I was traveling so much for work, she could never get ahold of me when she wanted to make changes.

So back to the table we went. In the year 2000, she introduced me to two investment vehicles I'd never heard of: *Index funds* and *exchange traded funds (ETF)*. Index funds are bought and sold when the market closes, and ETFs are traded like stocks on an exchange. Both mimic the indexes (carrying the exact stocks that are in a particular index, say the S&P 500 or the Russell 1000, for example), allowing me to be quite diversified at much lower fees than my managed funds. Best of all, these funds outperform over 85 percent of the high-priced managers, as illustrated by the following story.

In 2007, legendary investor Warren Buffett made a $1 million bet with a noted hedge fund manager. Buffet wagered that the Vanguard 500 Index Fund would outperform more sophisticated, high-priced hedge funds over a 10-year period. Guess who won? In 2017, the index fund returned 7.1 percent, while the basket of hedge funds returned 2.2 percent.

Strategy #3: Diversify

> *Diversify. In stocks and bonds, as in much*
> *else, there is safety in numbers.*
> —SIR JOHN TEMPLETON

I once saw a cartoon that cracked me up. A financial advisor sat across the desk from the Easter Bunny holding a basket of eggs. The advisor, leaning forward, warns the bunny sternly: "Never put all your eggs in one basket!"

The advisor, of course, was impressing on his client the importance of *diversification*, or spreading your money (eggs) into different asset classes (baskets), like stocks, bonds, cash, real estate, or maybe even commodities.

Furthermore, each asset class can be divided into sub-classes. For example:

- Stocks can be carved into small, medium, and large company stocks (otherwise known as small, medium, and large *cap* stocks).
- Bonds can be separated into corporate, municipal, and government bonds.
- Both stocks and bonds can be further subdivided into different regions, like the US, Europe, Asia, and emerging markets (underdeveloped countries).
- Real estate can be subdivided into raw land, residential, and commercial buildings.

The idea is that different asset classes or subclasses react differently to various conditions and time periods. So when, say, small cap stocks take a hit, large companies may be doing great. Or when US stocks are tanking, overseas companies may be holding their own, and emerging markets may be soaring—or vice versa. And since you never know which sector will take the next beating, diversification reduces the volatility of your whole portfolio.

In fact, a well-known study showed that diversification accounts for 93 percent of a portfolio's overall performance, 3 percent comes from stock picking, and 4 percent from luck. Index funds or ETFs make diversification easy and inexpensive.

How you diversify depends on your goals, which is why it's so important to have a plan. Let me remind you, a long-term diversified portfolio can mitigate many risks, but none of it matters if you can't keep your emotions in check.

Strategy #4: Time

The stock market is designed to transfer money from the active to the patient.
—WARREN BUFFETT

I'll never forget my first foray in the market. It was 1986, and I invested a small amount with a broker. A year later, October 1987, the market crashed, big-time! I called him in a panic, instructing him to sell everything. He begged me not to. I didn't listen. Of course, the market rebounded, quite quickly. I'd be a lot richer today had I stayed put.

Ten years later, almost to the day, in October 1997, the market took another nosedive. This time, I called my advisor, telling her to buy. I didn't see a crash. *I saw a sale!* Stock prices were cheap. I wouldn't need this money for at least 10 years. I trusted time would eventually reward my patience. And it certainly has.

As James Mackintosh, columnist for the *Wall Street Journal*, wrote, "Those who bought on the day the S&P 500 hit its top on Oct. 9, 2007, and held on through the subsequent panic and market collapse, have more than doubled their money. including dividends."[6]

If you were to look at a graph of the market over the past 100 years, you would see a jagged line resembling a roller coaster that, despite the dips and dives, keeps steadily climbing in an upward arc.

What I want you to remember: it's the overall direction, not the day-to-day bouncing, that matters. Those dips and dives only matter when you sell your holdings.

Here's how to use time to your advantage:

- **Money you'll need in the next 3 to 5 years** should be in cash (so you don't have to sell when the market is down).
- **Money you'll need in 5 to 10 years** can be in conservative stocks and bonds.
- **Money you won't need for 10+ years** can be in more volatile stocks, bonds, real estate, or commodities (because you have more time to ride out the highs and lows).

In 2016, *Marketwatch* reported: "There has literally never been a 20-year period in the past century or so that has resulted in a negative return for stocks, so investors with the patience and constitution to see their portfolio through a rough year should be rewarded regardless of the gloom and doom."

Trying to time the market, figuring out when it's reached it's high, selling because it's ready to fall, is a recipe for loss. Countless people have tried and failed. A few luck out, but never consistently. "After nearly 50 years in this business," wrote the late Jack Bogle, founder of Vanguard and creator of the first index fund, "I do not know of anybody who has timed the market successfully and consistently. I don't even know of anybody who knows anybody who has done it successfully and consistently."[7]

Strategy #5: Unplug

*Don't let the bearers of bad news become
the pallbearers of your happiness.*
—STEWART STAFFORD

Once you have these four strategies in place, I highly recommend that next time the market takes a tumble, you do this immediately: Turn off the TV. Shut down the computer. Don't look at your portfolio. Ignore the naysayers. Instead, take a walk or get a massage and remind yourself that the markets will go back up—because they always do.

This is what I'm doing and what I urge others to do while we are smack-dab in a global pandemic that, as of this writing, has yet to peak, creating unprecedented economic pandemonium. No one knows what the future holds. But if there's one lesson I've learned, and as I've warned earlier in this chapter, it is this: *Making decisions based on fear, greed, or any emotion is never a good strategy.* Instead, I'm doing a lot of yoga and taking long walks every day. Sometimes I'll call my advisor to check in. I don't think I could've approached this period with so little stress if I hadn't worked on rewiring my brain.

It's one thing to read about investing, but it's equally important to enhance your sense of self-efficacy and believe you can successfully build wealth over time. For this, we turn to Part II: "Rewiring," where you will learn how to rewire your brain for wealth and well-being. But before you go, take some time to fill out the Wealth Builder's Checklist, your guide for creating wealth.

Rewire in Action

Check the statements that are true for you. Let any statements left blank be the next steps you take to create wealth . . . and well-being.

☐ I am clear on my financial goals. They are:

_____

_____

_____

☐ I know my net worth. It is: _____

☐ I have no credit card debt. If I do, the total is: _____

☐ I have enough savings to support me for three to six months.
The amount is: _____

☐ I have money invested in a retirement account.
The amount is: _____

☐ I have investments outside a retirement account.
The amount is: _____

☐ I understand the investments I own.

☐ I will have enough money to support me in retirement.

☐ I have a will, power of attorney, and health directive.

☐ I feel assured that if I died today, my affairs would be properly handled.

☐ I know where all my financial documents and records are.

PART II

Rewiring

You are essentially who you create yourself to be, and all that occurs in your life is the result of your own making.
—STEPHEN RICHARDS

4

THE REWIRE RESPONSE

*Everyone thinks of changing the world, but
no one thinks of changing himself.*
—LEO TOLSTOY

THE THREE STEPS

You must unlearn what you've learned.
—YODA

In the previous section, we explored the four components needed to *Rewire for Wealth*—mind, body, spirit, and finances. Now let's put these pieces together and put them to work. I'm eager to introduce you to The Rewire Response, a three-step process to guide you toward achieving wealth and well-being. But, I have to warn you, this process, when consistently followed, will take you way beyond that single goal. You'll find yourself in a future far different from your past. You'll awaken to your authentic Self and the powerful being you truly are, before you were brainwashed to believe otherwise. And you'll know, with every fiber of your being, that you're truly safe because, at last, you trust yourself.

The Rewire Response I'm about to share has been greatly influenced by Dr. Jeffrey Schwartz's theory of self-directed neuroplasticity. Through extensive research, he proved that "willful mental effort generates a physical force that has the power to change the physical structure of the brain."[1] In other words, by deliberately monitoring what flows through your mind, you can virtually restructure your brain, reprogram your behavior, and resuscitate your true nature.

The Rewire Response consists of three steps that offer detailed directions for rewiring. They are:

- **Recognize**
- **Reframe**
- **Respond Differently**

In the next three chapters, I'll explain each step in greater depth.

Though the steps may seem simple, applying them is not. Rewiring is essentially an act of unlearning, a task that is tougher than it may sound.

"Unlearning is learning to think, behave, or perceive differently, when there are already beliefs, behaviors, or assumptions in place that get in the way," explains Marga Biller, project director of the Harvard Learning Innovations Laboratory.[2]

A Course in Miracles refers to unlearning as *"true learning . . . so that we can return to the full awareness of the Self that God created us to be."*[3]

I can tell you, without reservation, that if you're willing to do the work, you will be amazed at what happens.

THE NEED FOR CORRECTION

Discomfort is aroused only to bring the
need for correction into awareness.
—*A COURSE IN MIRACLES*

How do you know when it's time to rewire? Each of us has a highly sensitive internal sonar system. Whenever you feel bad, anything from mild distress to downright misery, your Soul's alerting you that something's amiss. As *A Course in Miracles* explains: *"All problems indicate an immediate correction is needed."* The Rewire Response provides the steps necessary to make those needed corrections.

THE FOUR PREMISES

Nothing will change unless it is understood.
—*A COURSE IN MIRACLES*

Before we go any further, I want you to understand the four premises on which The Rewire Response is based:

1. **Your brain is a product of your past.**
2. **What you focus your attention on gets wired in the brain.**
3. **Rewiring requires considerable effort, especially at the outset.**
4. **Unhealed trauma inhibits or undermines the rewiring process.**

Let me briefly explain what each premise means.

1. Your Brain Is a Product of Your Past

What you expect depends on what you've experienced.
—JASON ZWEIG

Your brain is like a scrapbook of past memories, reflecting the life you've lived and what you've learned. From the beginning of time and from the day of your birth, your brain's primary function was making sure you stayed out of harm's way (be it a poisonous snake or an angry parent) and that you lived to see another day (not being devoured by a predator or not losing your parents' love). Consequently, you developed guiding fictions, false narratives, and faulty beliefs leading you to engage in maladaptive behaviors you felt sure would keep you safe. Those fictions quickly became wired in your brain as facts, putting you on an endless hamster wheel of unhealthy habits.

2. What You Focus Your Attention on Gets Wired in the Brain

Tell me to what you pay attention to
and I will tell you who you are.
—JOSE ORTEGA Y GASSET

"The simple act of paying attention produces real and powerful physical changes in the brain," explains Dr. Schwartz.[4] Indeed, rewiring is a matter of deciding which thoughts, emotions, or stimuli you'll focus on while filtering out everything else. Whatever you give attention to strengthens those neuropathways. Whatever you ignore weakens them.

As the Course tells us: *"Each day, each hour, every instant, I am choosing what I want to look upon, the sounds I want to hear, the witnesses to what I want to be the truth for me."*

3. Rewiring Requires Considerable Effort, Especially at the Outset

All things are difficult before they are easy.
—THOMAS FULLER

Aligning your thoughts and feeling with a desired but not yet manifest outcome can feel like you're swimming against a raging current. As I said earlier, you're fighting the fierce gravitational pull of a well-worn pathway. Plus, you're experiencing actual chemical withdrawal from neuropeptides the old thoughts and emotions released in the brain. Inevitably, your Ego will gripe, *"This is too hard,"* insisting you return to the effortless flow of the familiar, onto the path of least resistance. You'll need to be highly motivated and wholly committed to defy your brain's hardwired habits and engage in healthier behaviors.

4. Unhealed Trauma Inhibits or Undermines the Rewiring Process

Trauma is personal. . . . When it is ignored or invalidated the silent screams continue internally heard only by the one held captive.
—DANIELLE BERNOCK

Rewiring is even harder, if not impossible, when you've experienced trauma. Anytime a situation evokes a painful event from your past, or a threat feels vaguely familiar, the brain secretes stress hormones, switching off the cerebral cortex, or logical brain, while activating the limbic system (the emotional fear center), firing off a string of warnings: *Stop! Proceed at your own peril! Dangerous conditions ahead!* It's not the actual situation, but how you remember it, that sets off your internal alarm system.

Trauma has many different faces. It could look like an emotionally distant mother, a sexually abusive relative, or watching someone you love suffer.

"Traumatized people chronically feel unsafe inside their bodies," explains Bessel A. van der Kolk, founder of the Trauma Center in Brookline, Massachusetts. "Their bodies are constantly bombarded by visceral warning signs, and, in an attempt to control these processes, they often become expert at ignoring their gut feelings and in numbing awareness of what is played out inside. They learn to hide from their selves."[5]

INCREASING MOTIVATION AND STRENGTHENING COMMITMENT

Motivation is what gets you started.
Commitment is what keeps you going.
—JIM ROHN

Your level of motivation determines your capacity to rewire. Because rewiring is demanding, unless you're extremely motivated, you'll be tempted to throw in the towel when the going gets tough. Or as Dr. John Arden states in his book *Rewire Your Brain*, "If you're not motivated to change, you'll just be going through the motions."[6]

But no matter how motivated you are, your drive will dissipate as you battle an old neuropathway's indefatigable, vicelike grip unless you're totally committed to stay the course. A commitment is a vow you make to yourself that you'll do whatever it takes to achieve your goal, even when resistance raises its ugly head, which it surely will. Once you commit fully, you can't possibly fail.

Actually, you're always committed to something—staying safe or staying true to yourself. Rewiring needs you to choose the latter—gathering the courage to venture beyond your stories, beyond your self-image, beyond your fears, beyond your family messages, and beyond the cultural conditioning, all the *shoulds*, *oughts*, and *musts* that served as your north star. You don't need to know all the how-tos or even believe it's possible. It doesn't matter. Once you make a commitment, the Universe revolves to help you reach your goal.

Rewire in Action

TAKING STOCK

Let's do a four-part exercise to assess and hopefully increase your level of motivation and commitment.

Part 1: Intention

> *All you need to do is ask yourself: Is this*
> *what I want to see? Do I want this?*
> —*A COURSE IN MIRACLES*

Begin by rewriting your intention for reading this book, as you did in Chapter 3, page 42. Doing this again helps because repetition is required to

(continued)

ensure cognitive rewiring. And your intention may have morphed at bit or changed completely.

My intention is: _____

_____

Now close your eyes, repeat your intention, then ask yourself the following questions. Take time to mull them over and really think about your responses, then jot down your answers.

Why do I want it? _____

_____

Why don't I want it? _____

_____

What if nothing changes? _____

_____

What if everything changes? _____

_____

Next, relax, take two deep breaths, and imagine you're sitting in beautiful surroundings. As you sit, imagine approaching four different parts of yourself—your *Inner Child* (you between 3 and 10 years old), your *Inner Adolescent* (you between 13 and 17 years old), your *Ego* (the voice of fear), and your *Future Self* (you one to five years from now).Separately, tell each one your intention and ask what each one thinks. Visualize each pondering the question and replying truthfully.

What does my Child say? _____

_____

What does my Adolescent say? _____

_____

What does my Ego say? _____

_____

What does my Future Self say? _____

_____

Finally, reflect on this inquiry with these four parts of you. Then ask yourself this final question:

Why will I let myself achieve my intention? _____

_____

Part 2: Motivation

> *Increasing motivation for change in the learner*
> *is all the teacher need do to guarantee change.*
> **—A COURSE IN MIRACLES**

Next, let's rate your level of motivation on a scale of 1 (not at all) to 5 (completely, totally).

How driven am I to achieve my intention? My motivation is at

_____ (Be honest!)

If you aren't at 5, ask yourself:

Why don't I want it? _____

_____

(continued)

What am I scared of? _____

_____

Part 3: Commitment

> *You cannot be totally committed sometimes.*
> —*A COURSE IN MIRACLES*

Now rate your level of commitment to achieving your intention on a 1–5 scale. How determined am I to walk through fire to make it happen? ____

Anything less than a 5 means only one thing. You're not committed. Just as you can't be a little bit pregnant, so you can't be a little bit committed. You either are or you aren't. And as I mentioned before, you are, in fact, committed to something. In this case, either to repeating the past or rewiring for a new future.

Part 4: The Oath

> *When confronted with a challenge, the committed heart will search for a solution. The undecided heart searches for an escape.*
> —ANDY ANDREWS

What if you're a 4 or less and you'd like to raise the number? I invite you to work on strengthening your resolve by taking what I call *The Oath of Commitment*, a series of statements (which you can see below) that are meant to be sacred promises you make to yourself. Even if they don't ring true right now, say the following statements aloud or in your head. Then use them as affirmations, repeating some or all of them every morning, throughout the day, and again before bed. Even if you're a solid 5, I urge you to do the same. Repeating these statements will be your first step in actively training your mind to rewire your brain.

- *I am committed* to owning my power, becoming all I can be, because, honestly, that's what wealth building forces me to do.
- *I am committed* to increasing my net worth, no matter how loud that little voice in my head screams, *Stop, don't do it!*
- *I am committed*, even if right now, at this moment, I have no idea how I'm going to do it. It doesn't matter. I know the Universe will guide me toward my goal.
- *I am committed* to stop telling my old story, with all the *shoulds*, *oughts*, and *musts* that have calcified into hardwired rules I must live by.
- *I am committed* to seeing my excuses for what they are: smoke screens to hide the truth—I'm scared to change.
- *I am committed* to face my fears by taking baby steps because I know that the moment I commit, fear will rear its ugly head.
- *I am committed* to challenge myself to think in new ways about new things, retraining my mind to physically alter my brain and thus create new habits.
- *I am committed* because I understand that every time I don't keep a commitment or I break a promise to myself, I erode my self-esteem and self-efficacy, losing confidence in myself.
- *I am committed* to getting back up every time I fall off the wealth-building wagon. This is not about being perfect. It's about being persistent.
- *I am committed* to asking for and receiving support. Wealth building is not a do-it-yourself project.

Bonus Points: Commit not just to yourself but share your intention with a trusted friend or loved one. Ask that person for support in holding you accountable. You can do the same in return. Perhaps both of you, or more if you want, could form a support group to study this book.

Remember, at any given moment you have a choice in how to respond: Repeat or Rewire. Now, turn the page, and you'll start to learn how to make sure you choose The Rewire Response every time.

STEP #1: RECOGNIZE

*Recognize—verb—to acknowledge or
take notice of in some definite way.*
—*MERRIAM-WEBSTER DICTIONARY*

PATRICIA'S STORY, PART ONE

*Many of us will not realize who we are
because we do not believe in ourselves.*
—SUNDAY ADELAJA

Patricia Vitera is a comptroller for a construction firm who
joined my Rewire Mentorship Program when she was struggling financially after a painful divorce.

"I want to have money work for me, to be confident in
investing," she said in a soft Texas drawl. "But I'm not making progress. I keep hitting roadblocks."

It was only our second session, yet she was obviously irritated.

"I've been doing a lot of work and making small changes. But I'm frustrated," she lamented. "I want big changes, big leaps." She paused, sighed heavily, and added. "Rewiring is just so hard for me."

"Oh honey, I promise, it's hard for everyone, particularly at the beginning," I assured her "Keep in mind you've just begun." Then I asked her to describe a small change she'd made. It took her a few minutes to think of one.

"Well, just this weekend, I was thinking about my ex-husband and how I didn't feel like I deserved someone better. And then I caught myself and said 'Whoa! Wait a minute! No, no, no! That's my old story.'"

I wanted to jump through the phone line and hug her. "You did it," I squealed. "You took the first step in rewiring. You recognized an old belief for what it was, a big lie. How did that feel?"

"It actually felt really good to realize." I could almost hear her smile

But I sensed her smile vanish with my next questions. "Why did you dismiss that insight as small? Why didn't you appreciate that this was progress? You've heard the saying: what you appreciate, appreciates."

"I'm always doubting myself. I don't have any confidence," she said ruefully. "I don't know when the last time I said to myself, 'Well done, Patsy.'"

Her massive insecurity kept the seed of a new story—*I deserve better*—from taking root in her brain. Yet her reaction made perfect sense. Our human brains are predisposed toward noticing negativity, a necessity for self-preservation.

That's what kept our ancestors safe just as it did my client from her abusive father.

But dwelling on the negative is a form of brain abuse known as *rumination*. Like a cow chewing its cud, she kept chewing on what she didn't do and how bad she felt, which, of course, triggered spasms of self-doubt, further strengthening that already deeply carved cognitive path.

"Would you like to rewire your self-doubt so you can start appreciating small strides?" I asked, sensing she was ready. "Every time you don't appreciate a small change you made, you're just reinforcing the old wiring of not good enough."

"Yes," she declared. "I'm at the point where I want those old stories gone and the new ones to begin. But it's hard."

"Yes, it's hard. But let me make it simple for you," I offered. "Let's focus solely on the first step."

And that, dear reader, is exactly where you and I will begin—with Step 1: *Recognize*. To simplify it even further, I've broken this step into four phases:

Phase I: Observe without judgment.

Phase II: React with curiosity (or congratulations).

Phase III: Separate your thoughts from yourself.

Phase IV: Blame your brain.

The point of this process is to engage the cerebral cortex (the rational brain) and disengage the limbic system (the emotional fear center). I like to think of this step as a mental spam filter, notifying you of any unsolicited, unwanted, and unhealthy thoughts so you can ignore them.

PHASE I: OBSERVE WITHOUT JUDGMENT

*Sometimes when we judge ourselves we really put
a wrench in the healing process, don't we?*

—JODI AMAN

The National Science Foundation declares that every day about 50,000 thoughts float through your head like bits of dust you barely notice. Of those thoughts, 80 percent are negative and 95 percent are repetitive.[1]

And this is exactly where we start rewiring for wealth—by paying attention to those passing thoughts, particularly the negative and repetitive ones. Only when you become aware of your thoughts do you have the power to change them.

Dr. Schwartz discovered that when his OCD patients observed their sensations, their urges and impulses, they were able to "strengthen their capacity to resist the insistent thought of OCD."[2]

And that's all the first phase of the first step asks you to do: *Notice what you're thinking, feeling, and doing, particularly if it doesn't feel good.*

Patricia seemed surprised it was that simple. "So when fear or doubt or inadequacy walks into my brain, I just notice it?" she said. "That's all?"

"Yep. That's the first thing you do," I replied, adding one stipulation. "Do *not* judge anything as good or bad. Just notice impassively."

The point of Phase I is to witness your internal dialogue as if you were an impartial spectator or objective bystander, viewing yourself from a distance. Maybe you remember a scene in the movie *Annie Hall* when Diane Keaton literally steps out of her body to observe her interaction with Woody Allen. She simply watches what unfolds. That's what this first phase is asking you to do. Just take note of your thoughts and feelings. Do not dwell on, criticize, or analyze what you notice. And don't overthink or shame yourself. Simply recognize when any of the following happen.

- You're feeling scared, frustrated, anxious, inadequate, or unhappy.
- You're telling your old story: "There's never enough." "I always doubt myself." "I have to hide who I really am." "I'm such a klutz with money."
- You're replaying old patterns like not opening bills, eating when anxious, overdrawing an account, or constantly needing to control.
- You have a strong negative reaction or an emotional upset.
- You're beating yourself up or putting yourself down.
- You're pessimistic about your ability to change based on past experiences.
- You're listening to your Ego (the voice of fear) because it always speaks first, screams loudest, and *never* shuts up.
- You're responding in a healthier way. (It's important to acknowledge progress.)

PHASE II: REACT WITH CURIOSITY (OR CONGRATULATIONS)

Be curious, not judgmental.

—WALT WHITMAN

As you become aware of your uncomfortable or undesirable thoughts or feelings, Phase II asks that you react with what Dr. Richard O'Connor, in his book *Rewire*, calls "compassionate curiosity."[3] In other words, respond not with self-recrimination but with inquisitiveness, saying to yourself evenly, calmly: "Isn't that interesting?" or "Oh, look what I'm doing."

I loved how Jessica Bensley, a member of my Rewire Mentorship Program, described her experience with Phase II. "On my walk this morning, I was listening to my mind chatter. It was so fascinating being the observer observing my thoughts," she told me. "I recognized that 98 percent of my thoughts are founded in some kind of judgment. That was so interesting. Here I was thinking I was the love child of peace and joy!"

As she began to notice that "chatter," rather than judge herself harshly, Jessica was intrigued by her discovery. I suggest you do the same. Recognize any detrimental, distressing, or disparaging thoughts with both detachment and fascination: "Oh isn't that interesting."

Or, if you notice a healthy reaction that makes you feel better, congratulate yourself for making headway. The more you appreciate your progress, the quicker you'll wire that into your brain.

PATRICIA'S STORY PART TWO

The best way out is always through.
—ROBERT FROST

"The message I'm getting is to acknowledge my old story. Recognize I'm in it," she said. "But what about all the bitterness, anger and hurt that comes up with that old story? I feel that's my weakest link. I automatically regress to the old wiring." She was referring to her alcoholic father's abuse and her ex-husband's gaslighting.

I assured her that staying mindful but impassive is not easy, and here's why: Unhealed pain triggers stress hormones preparing your brain for impending doom. However, trying to stifle the hurt only strengthens it.

"Don't fight your feelings," I urged her. "Stay with the sensations no matter how uncomfortable, as long as you can. Recognize this is an opportunity to heal, to finally release the pain rather than repress it which you've always done."

As Neuropsychiatrist Dr. Jeffrey Schwartz explains: "Emotions should be felt and constructively dealt with because they honor your true needs."[4]

In his book, *The Brain: The Story of You*, David Eagleman shared an experiment where participants watched a sad movie. Half were told to respond normally. The other half were told to suppress their emotions. Afterward, they were all given a hand exerciser and told to squeeze it as long and hard as they could. Those who suppressed their emotions gave up sooner. The reason: emotional repression is exhausting and drains your energy for other things.[5]

It's highly likely that suppressed emotions will emerge in this process for you, too. Rather than shove them down, let them bob to the surface. Hear what those feelings have to say. Give yourself permission to be angry at your parents or spouse or former best friend for how they treated you. You have a right to be enraged. Or hurt. Or humiliated. Or saddened. Similarly, recognize these feelings may be driving you to engage in acts of self-sabotage, like avoiding your finances or distrusting your decisions.

Remind yourself that this is your Ego, the voice of fear, which always speaks first and loudest. It wants nothing more than for you to numb your feelings with various diversions. But whatever you suppress, grows stronger.

As reported in the *Wall Street Journal*, "Research shows that suppression activates the [part of the brain] where your body's flight or fight response resides. Suppression will make you more anxious in the long run and will have harmful effects on your health."[6]

If you can let the feelings flow through you, without judgment or censorship, they'll eventually dissipate, allowing you to connect with your Soul's wisdom.

PHASE III: SEPARATE YOUR THOUGHTS FROM YOURSELF

Believe you can. Believe you can't.
Either way you'll be right.
—HENRY FORD

After you observe without judgment and react with curiosity (or congratulations), I want you to start Phase III and draw a distinction between you and your thoughts. When you notice yourself thinking, "I don't trust myself," shift to "Oh, I'm having a thought about not trusting myself." Or instead of "I'm scared," try "I am having a fearful thought." Similarly, rather than "I have to buy those gorgeous boots," say to yourself, "I'm having a thought about buying those boots."

"Thoughts are not truth," writes Dr. Schwartz. "Instead of reacting to these thoughts and feelings as 'these are me,' regard them as events in the mind that can be considered and examined."[7]

The idea is to create some distance between your Ego's warped distortions, your brain's old programs, and your automatic urge to act on either or both. Simply recognize that you're having a thought but acknowledge that you are *not* your thoughts. Nor are these thoughts true. They are guiding fictions, false narratives, deeply rutted and well-worn neural pathways that have been strongly reinforced over your lifetime. They are implanted beliefs, not genuine facts. When you recognize them for what they are—indoctrinated ideas—you can begin to weaken them by challenging them.

For example, during a tough negotiation, my client Joyce Griggs, a strategist for pharmaceutical firms, felt her throat start to constrict and was ready to back down.

Instead, she told me, "I literally talked to myself. I said, 'OK. Take a step back and just witness what's happening. I'm having a negative reaction. This is an old neuropathway that's playing itself out, and I can honor it for what it is. This reaction may have served me in the past when it was better not to speak up. But that's not necessary anymore. I need to rewire this.'" She took a deep breath, quickly reframed (which is Step #2, which we'll discuss in the next chapter) and continued the conversation without missing a beat.

Perhaps my favorite example of separating from your thoughts came from my client Amy who told me how she personified her fear. "I call fears my little warriors and imagine them as little boys dressed up as warriors who need a hug. They're always there. But they're not as raucous as they were." You've got to give her credit for creativity.

PHASE IV: BLAME YOUR BRAIN

There is hope, even when your brain tells you there isn't.
—JOHN GREEN

Once his OCD patients observed their impulses, Dr. Schwartz instructed them to "reattribute those thoughts and urges to pathological brain circuitry" that "reflects a malfunction of [the] brain, not a real need."

Within a week, he said, "they reported the disease was no longer controlling them and could do something about it."

Though your circuits may not be "pathological," they are definitely defectively wired, generating such beliefs as *I am not enough* or *I can't do anything right*. Recognize that these words are, according to Dr. Schwartz, nothing more than the toxic waste from the brain . . . and the Ego.

Instead of criticizing yourself—*Oh damn it. I'm spending too much again*—realize, "Oh I'm spending because that's the way my brain is wired. That's what my dad did when he was stressed."

PATRICIA'S STORY PART THREE

A choice causes one brain state to be
activated rather than another.

—JEFFREY SCHWARTZ

The next time I talked to Patricia, she was fretting about her finances, fed up with her situation.

"I've worked hard and put my life on hold just to get ahead. I should have more money. I should be farther ahead. But there's never enough. Never."

"Every time you say *I should*, that's a sign you're in Ego, who's full of lies," I warned her, sharing what my friend singer-songwriter Athena Burke always says: "Anything after *I should* is a lie." Patricia liked that.

I suggested we take a look at her finances and figure out the truth. As she ticked off the exact amount in each account, I was struck by how financially diligent she'd been, how well diversified she was, and how much she'd saved. She actually had more than enough for retirement, though clearly, she couldn't see it.

"You've done a great job," I exclaimed.

"The financial planner I went to a few months ago told me the same thing," Patricia admitted sheepishly. "She said I'm not behind. I'm doing OK. She opened a window so I could see that."

"Why did you close that window again?" I inquired.

"You know," she said pensively, "I never feel there's enough. Which were the exact words my parents used. We never had enough."

"Exactly!" I told her. "It's not the truth. It's how your brain is *wired*. You can only see what confirms your long-held belief, 'There's never enough.' But now that you understand where that belief originated, you'll need to rewire that belief before you can own the truth."

PAYING ATTENTION TO THE POSITIVE

You do not need to pay attention to those
voices within you that create pain, or make
you feel less competent, smart, or able.

—SANAYA ROMAN

Up until now, we've been mostly focusing on your internal dialogue when it's negative. But your Soul's soft whispers need to be heard and heeded too. In order to strengthen the more desirable yet still weak neuropathways, it's important to recognize positive experiences and positive feelings. Like Patricia's brief recognition that she'd done a good job with her money or when she realized she deserved better than an abusive man. Or the experience I had with Joyce Griggs when she came to my home in Port Townsend, Washington, for a full day of coaching at a VIP Rewire Intensive.

"I am at the end of my rope," Joyce said, explaining that she'd just been fired from her pharmaceutical job and her marriage was falling apart. Though she was highly stressed about her future, she had the wisdom and depth of a woman who'd obviously done a lot of work on herself. She wasted no time diving in deep. I liked her immediately.

After an intense morning of exploration, we took a lunch break at a local restaurant where we enjoyed the view of sailboats gliding lazily by and the majestic Olympic Mountains in the background. It was a beautiful sunny day. We were relaxed and nibbling on our salads when she calmly blurted out, apropos to nothing, "I want to be a nomad." She laughed in amazement. "I have no idea where that come from."

Joyce could easily have dismissed that thought as a silly slip of tongue, but she chose to pay attention. We both felt those words came straight from her Soul and carried a kernel of truth. As we talked, it began to make sense. She loved to travel. And she'd severed all ties keeping her in one place. She decided to keep an open mind and look for signs.

The very next week she was headed to Texas for a conference. While attending the event, she met a lot of interesting people. But two in particular made a strong impression.

"I exchanged business cards with a woman whose company was located in Greece," she told me later. "I noticed I was very taken by this."

That same day she met another woman. "When I asked her where she was based, she said, 'Well I'm a nomad.' I got the shivers."

On the plane from Austin, Joyce disclosed, "I noticed a little voice in my head kept telling me to go to Athens. I thought to myself, 'Huh? That is crazy. What do you mean, go to Athens?' I'd never been. I didn't know anyone there. It didn't make sense."

Again, she could easily have ignored that voice. "But I found myself booking flights for two weeks later," she said.

Soon after she arrived in Athens, Joyce attended a yoga class, met an American woman, and they went for coffee afterward. "This woman told me her story about how she was called to Athens, had never been, but something was pushing her to go. And I thought to myself, 'Oh my gosh, she's telling my story.'"

That was over a year ago, and Joyce has been traveling nonstop, building a business as a strategist to pharmaceutical firms ever since. She's returned to Greece several times. "The woman I had met in yoga class connected me with her whole community," Joyce said with obvious delight. "I've found my tribe. I'm pretty certain I'll move there in the next year or so. My financial advisor is going through the numbers now to see if I can swing it."

She later told me that her advisor gave her the go-ahead and she set a date to move to Greece. There was no way, sitting in my guesthouse, Joyce could have come up with this plan. Instead, she paid attention to her intuitive nudges and positive reactions to seemingly chance occurrences and, as she put it, "I just started following the breadcrumbs."

The eminent neuroscientist Michael M. Merzenich, professor emeritus at the University of California, San Francisco, once said: "We choose and sculpt how our ever-changing minds will work. We choose who we will be the next moment."[8]

So, go ahead, think about who you want to be and what you want to do as you turn the page and get ready for Step #2.

6

STEP #2: REFRAME

WHAT IS REFRAMING?

You cannot choose what the world should be.
But you can choose how you would see it.
—*A COURSE IN MIRACLES*

The first step in The Rewire Response was somewhat passive, asking only that you observe your thoughts or feelings with curiosity and without judgment. This second step, however, requires mental discipline. Once you recognize an unwanted or negative thought, you need to *Reframe* it. Reframing means deliberately choosing whether you will view an event or situation through the eyes of your eternally fearful Ego, desperate to protect you, or through the lens of your loving

Soul who knows you're safe and wants you to shine. This choice, albeit challenging, will be life changing.

"Your ability to redirect your thinking," the Course exclaims, *"is the most powerful device that was ever given you for change."*

Reframing—shifting your perception from fear to love, from negative judgment to compassionate acceptance—is how you literally create miracles. Simply put, every time you redirect your mind to regard something from a more tolerant or positive perspective your world will miraculously change.

The truth is, you or I never respond to what is actually going on in the moment, only to our interpretation of it. And your interpretation is inevitably based on your past experience, much like navigating life through the rearview mirror.

Neuroscience explains quite clearly that your interpretation of the world you see is but a reflection of how your brain's been wired. And many physicists, like David Bohm, would agree: "The ability to perceive or think differently is more important than the knowledge gained."[1]

In actuality, none of us sees the unvarnished truth about anything, only our own version of it. And our version's been highly polluted by our previous experiences, flawed learning, imprecise memories, painful wounds, and mistaken beliefs. Our recollections of prior events have little to do with what *really* happened but only reflects our "story" about what happened. As we learned in Chapter 2, the law of cause and effect states that nothing out there has anything to do with how you feel. It's only your thoughts about it.

In order to reframe, you first need to recognize your unhealthy thoughts (Step #1). I once read an interview with the actress and activist Jane Fonda, who described how she finally reframed an unrelenting belief. "I spent so much of my life feeling that if I'm not perfect, no one can love me," she said. "Then I realized . . . sometimes good enough is good enough."

Coming to that conclusion, she divulged, was not an easy journey. Indeed, reframing can be extremely challenging and takes concerted effort due to what scientists call *inattentional blindness*. Our long-held beliefs cast impenetrable shadows over our perceptions, blinding us to other interpretations that may be blatantly obvious to others.

HOW DO YOU REFRAME?

The moment you change your perception is the moment you rewrite the chemistry of your body.
—DR. BRUCE H. LIPTON

Long ago, when hungry predators were a constant threat, we relied on fear for our survival. But times have changed, and so has fear's function. Nowadays, fear is rarely a sign your life is at stake. But it still serves a vital role. Fear, explains the Course, *"brings the need for correction forcibly into awareness."* That means whenever you feel even a shred of fear or any uncomfortable sensation, rather than instinctively recoiling, consider it a valuable warning that you're following the wrong thought system—your Ego's. It's time to reframe and choose to follow the Soul's loving wisdom by focusing on your dreams and desires instead of rehashing your tales of woe.

Just as in the first step, to reframe you must suspend judgment. Nothing that happens is good or bad, positive or negative, right or wrong. Everything, no matter how upsetting, is a gift for your growth, a lesson to learn, or a message from Spirit. Every unpleasant experience is, in reality, an opportunity to rewire.

Reframing is what psychologists call *selective attention*, which I define as consciously selecting to focus your attention on one thing while ignoring everything else.

"The seemingly simple function of paying attention produces real and powerful physical change in the brain," explains Dr. Jeffrey Schwartz.[2] "When your focus of attention shifts, so do patterns of brain activity."

And when that happens, as they say in neuroscience circles, "neurons that are out of synch fail to link."

You may remember the classic image of the lady in the first figure. What do you see—the old woman or the young one?

Or how about the picture in the second figure? Do you see the duck or the rabbit?

As you stare at each picture, notice you can choose to see one or the other, but not both at the same time. What you see is determined by what you pay attention to. And you have the power to direct your mind to choose which one you'll concentrate on. That goes for the optical illusions in these two pictures, as well as invoking optimistic thoughts over depressing ones or contemplating the possibility of success over the prospect of failure. You have free will, or more specifically what Dr. Schwartz refers to as *free won't*, the mind's veto power over the brain's commands.[3]

Corporate consultant and former client Michele Phillips described this quite poignantly: "I saw a bum on the street and said to myself, 'that's possible.' Then I saw a beautiful mansion and said, 'that's possible too.' Anything's possible, right? It's up to me to decide what I want to focus on."

"Developing greater control over your attention is perhaps the single most powerful way to shape your brain," psychologist Rick Hanson wrote in *Buddha's Brain*.[4] In fact, neuroplasticity, our ability to change our brain, is impossible without focused attention.

The act of reframing is nothing short of a superpower that everyone has, yet few actually recognize or put into practice.

Wherever you direct your attention, consistently, over a period of time, will become your reality. The frontal, rational brain will automatically filter out anything you're not paying attention to. Reframing is the taproot for transformation, the cornerstone for rewiring, and the foundation for creating miracles.

There are two ways to redirect your attention: overtly, by shifting what you focus your eyes on, or covertly, by internally replacing a thought or feeling with a different one.

Overt Reframing

We become what we behold.
—DEAN BROWN

My client Emma had built a wildly popular event business that never made a profit. She was so passionate about her work and eager to rapidly expand the business that she neglected to keep an eye on the bottom line. As expenses began exceeding revenues, instead of cutting costs, she maxed out her credit and brought on investors, accruing massive debt.

When she joined my Rewire Mentorship Program, she'd changed her business model to corporate consulting. It was far more lucrative, she explained, "but every last penny is going toward debt." I could hear the anguish in her voice.

"I need to know how I can bring in more money," she pleaded, eager to figure out how to ratchet up her income so she could pay down her debt. But I wanted to slow her down, help her rewire. I suspected that no matter how much she earned, she'd continue to create financial instability, just like her dad, who always made a lot of money but spent even more.

"I've done a lot of work on myself. I was in therapy for 11 years," she said. "I know I've been reliving my dad's relationship with money. I'm scared I can't escape this pattern."

"Let's lift the hood and see what's under that fear, shall we?" I suggested, then asked her a question she didn't expect. "What if you *were* wealthy? How would that feel? What would it look like?" Her homework was to sit with those questions.

At our next appointment she said, "For the last two weeks, I kept repeating the mantra: *I am a wealthy woman.* It brought a lot of stuff up. I had a lot of feelings. I just sat with them, noticing."

She was surprised, shocked really, at what emerged. "I saw a lonely old woman, dried up, worn out, wearing a mink coat, driving a Cadillac, all alone. It was nauseating."

"Isn't that interesting?" I said. "Can you see why you're repeating your father's pattern?"

"I always equated money with confinement and limitation. I made some bad decisions. Now I feel like a failure."

"You're not a failure," I assured her. "You acted on an unconscious decision you made long ago that acting responsibly would set you up for limitation. And having more than you needed would leave you lonely and bitter. The brain will only do and see what confirms its beliefs. Let's rewire that, shall we?"

"Yes!" she exclaimed. "I want to reenvision myself being wealthy as a grounding experience, allowing me to have full expression."

Her homework was to find a way to reframe her belief. She did it by overtly reframing, or intentionally looking for more appealing examples.

"I started searching for wealthy women, and I found some who are super juicy, engaged in the community, and aren't burned out or dried up. I've started saying, 'That's what a wealthy woman looks like.' And you know, it's working. I've consciously put a different face on her."

As soon as she overtly reframed her image of a wealthy woman, by purposely seeking role models who were the opposite of her initial assumption, it was rather amazing what happened next. She began seeing things at work she hadn't noticed before: The outrageous bill from her longtime book-keeper, for the same amount she'd been paying for years, yet she never questioned the high fee before. The line of credit she could easily pay off, saving her hundreds of dollars in interest payment, but it never occurred to her until now. She knew what she needed to do. Her focus had automatically shifted from fear of limitation and loneliness to excitement about taking responsibility.

Covert Reframing

I can elect to change all thoughts that hurt.
—A COURSE IN MIRACLES

We met Patricia in the previous chapter when she was worried about not having enough. Even after we reviewed her finances and I pointed out she was in a great place financially (a financial professional had told her the same thing), she wasn't able to own the truth nor calm her panic. Evidently overt reframing, looking at external facts, didn't work for her.

"Patricia," I said firmly, "We both know your brain's been wired to see only scarcity. But I want you to look at these numbers. I want you to recognize the truth of what's here. And it's not lack, not even close."

She took a few moments to study the numbers, and you could've knocked me over with a feather by what she said next. "I just heard this small voice say to me, 'Dang, girl, you got it together.'" She wasn't able to reframe tangible evidence, but she did a great job covertly reframing her worrisome thoughts with thoughts of appreciation.

I grabbed onto her words and led her straight into Step #2. "Wonderful, Patricia. Now it's your choice," I said. "Which voice are you going to follow? The voice of the frightened little Ego insisting you don't have enough. Or your quiet but adoring Soul giving you a big high five, saying, 'Dang girl you got it together.' Do you really want to continue to stress over a hardwired brain circuit or are you ready to rejoice in the fact you have more than enough?"

When she didn't respond, I gently asked how she was feeling.

"I'm grinning inside," she chirped. "I feel confident. I recognize I have a choice in how I think. I know I'm capable of change. I'm capable of rewiring. When old thoughts come up, I can redirect them. When I catch myself on a downward spiral, I can say, 'Wait, I have a choice. I'm ok.'" Patricia gives us a stunning example of covertly reframing by tuning into her inherent wisdom even if she was unable to intellectually process the positive numbers.

When you rewire for wealth, it's not just your finances that get stronger. You'll notice how powerful you've become.

I define a powerful woman as *someone who knows who she is, knows what she wants, and expresses that in the world, unapologetically.* And when you fully step into your power, you'll discover your true self hidden under the lead blanket of misguided neuropathways.

SEVEN TECHNIQUES FOR REFRAMING

We don't see the world as it is. We see the world as we are.

—ANAÏS NIN

As I've said, reframing isn't easy. There will be times when, try as you might, you just can't seem to shift your perspective. Jeffrey Schwartz coined the term "brain lock" to describe when "our impulse laden brain" prevents us from moving on to the next thought or feeling.[5] It's true, certain visceral cravings, sensations, compulsions, or impulses—like those irresistible urges to spend without restraint or the familiar ache of feeling inferior—can seem impossible to stop. We've literally become addicted to the neurotransmitters, or chemicals, that those thoughts release in our brain. Consequently, we're compelled to repeat unwanted behaviors to reduce the tension of chemical withdrawal. But the relief is short lived. Sometimes, especially if this has become a chronic pattern, the only successful resolution is a therapeutic intervention like EMDR or a 12-step group like Debtors Anonymous.

However, here are seven techniques I've learned from clients and my own experience that may help you reframe when you're struggling to do so.

● Rewire in Action ●

MY REFRAME

Write down one negative thought, feeling, or behavior you recognized in the last chapter that you want to rewire.

_____

_____

As you read through the seven techniques, jot down some ideas for reframing your negative thought, feeling, or behavior.

_____

_____

_____

_____

1. Go to Gratitude

> *Be thankful for what you have. You'll end up*
> *having more. If you concentrate on what you*
> *don't have, you will never have enough.*
>
> **—OPRAH**

I will never forget, a few years ago, when I could not, for the life of me, reframe a sudden onslaught of shame. I'd just given what I thought was a very engaging talk to a large group of women. The person in charge of the event came rushing up to me but, to my surprise, criticized my response to an audience member's question. I honestly felt she was overreacting and brushed off her words like an annoying piece of lint.

But as soon as I crawled into bed that night, her comments hit me like a gut punch, sending me spiraling down a black hole of shame. I felt sick to my stomach, certain everyone saw I was a fraud. My pain, like a blindfold, blocked my ability to see things differently. I couldn't reframe these horrible feeling. This went on for hours. Then, out of the blue, an image of my three daughters popped in my head. Knowing it's impossible to feel love and fear at the same time, I deliberately switched my attention to the enormous love and gratitude I have for my girls. I stayed with that gratitude until my heart swung wide open and a sense of calm washed over me, gently dissolving the shame. I fell into a deep sleep. The next morning the woman who criticized me greeted me with a big hug and thanked me for a wonderful event. Go figure!

2. Find Compassion

Whatever brought you pain see how it's been your teacher.
—*A COURSE IN MIRACLES*

I was quite moved during my first coaching session with Patti Fagan, a successful money coach, who had a horrific childhood. Her mother got pregnant, never knowing who the father was.

"The message I took from that was I shouldn't be here. My mom was ashamed of me. So I had all of this shame, and it was showing up massively in credit card debt."

By the time Patti joined Rewire, she was debt-free and financially secure, which she attributes to years in therapy.

But she was eager to rewire her crushing fear of rejection. "I realized I had so much practice feeling rejected because it kept getting reaffirmed by my memories of my mom," she recalled.

I told her to notice when she felt shame and rejection. As she observed her feelings, she recognized how much sorrow and anguish she carried. "I told you that I had a PhD in suffering, and you said, 'No, you have a PhD in overcoming adversity.' And I went, 'Oh my God, that's true. It's what made me who I am and like something to be proud of.'"

In that moment, Patti recognized that if feeling unwanted was wired in, it could be wired out. "But I knew that it was such a strong message I couldn't just be passive about it." So, every time she thought about being rejected, she reframed by focusing on having compassion for her mom.

"I've come to see that my mother represents generations of dysfunction. Her mother gave her away when she was five years old. She never got the nurturing she needed. That gave me so much compassion for her, and I realized that she's just a product of her own upbringing."

Then Patti discovered compassion for herself.

"I've had several therapists say they're surprised I'm not a heroin addict," Patti recalled. "But I feel by the grace of God, I didn't go that route. I didn't seek to numb the pain and beat myself up. I just had a drive to heal. I feel like God chose me in the generational line to be the one that has this hunger, this desire to seek a better way."

I loved how she reframed her past with an affirmation: *God chose me.* "Rejection is no longer my life story," she explained. "Now it's 'I'm chosen.'"

When I interviewed her much later for this book, her reframe had been hardwired. "The difference between where I am now and where I started is that I feel like I can't possibly believe I could be rejected now. Like there's no way you can convince me today that I'll be rejected."

3. Pose a Question

At least I can decide I do not like what I feel
now. I want another way to look at this.
Perhaps there's another way to look at this?
—*A COURSE IN MIRACLES*

Asking yourself pointed questions can help redirect your attention. Try simple questions like these:

- How would I rather feel?
- What's a kinder, gentler way to view this?
- Where can I focus my attention that would make me happier?
- What do I want to wire in my brain?
- Why don't I replace this thought with a more loving one?
- Would I rather feel peace instead of this anger/upset?

Whenever I have trouble reframing, I repeat a lesson from the Course, saying it as a prayer: *"Above all, how can I see this differently?"* I always share this with clients.

Holly Gossett is an energy healer and spiritual seeker who also cleans houses, including mine. It broke my heart to see how financially illiterate she was, so I invited her to join my

Rewire Mentorship program. She wholeheartedly accepted, hungry to learn.

Just as I was working on this chapter, Holly came rushing into my office.

"We found a new house. It's so much bigger, so full of light. It's perfect," she enthused, then quickly grew quiet. "The problem is it's twice what we pay in rent. Last night, I'm lying in bed, my body full of tension. I was frozen in the feeling of 'We can't afford it.' I felt like I was having a panic attack. I knew the fear was clouding my ability to see clearly."

She tried to calm down but to no avail, until she remembered to specifically ask: 'How can I see this differently?' The fear didn't subside right away, but her mind apparently began searching for solutions. Suddenly she had a flash of clarity. "Oh my gosh," she realized, "I have enough in savings to make up the difference in what we needed."

Until she joined my program, Holly never had savings. "For the first time, I know what it's like to have more than enough. I've never had that feeling before. Money always flowed in, but I never let it accumulate to use for a purpose." She, her husband, and their daughter are now living happily, peacefully in their spacious new house.

4. Take a Break

Taking a break can lead to breakthroughs.
—RUSSELL ERIC DOBDA

Another client of mine, Michele Phillips, is a high-energy, upbeat executive coach, corporate trainer, and author who admitted, "Sometimes I have no trouble reframing my crappy feelings in the moment, but other times I just can't." When she has difficulty, she told me, "I have to disconnect from my thoughts, do something different, sooth myself until I feel better." She'll color in a coloring book, write in her journal, ride her bike, or go for a swim.

"When I come back it's easier to choose a different thought pattern."

Michele gave me an example. She'd recently gone on a fabulous European bike trip with her husband and friends. A few days after their arrival, her husband had an accident and needed to fly home. It was a long flight, and he upgraded to first class while she sat in the back.

"I was fine, I was sitting in the back all happy, not even worrying about anything, and then I went up to see him, and I got viscerally angry when I saw how classy his accommodations and meal service were.

"I went back to my seat fuming, and I'm thinking, 'Oh my God, Michele, the poor guy has a hurt leg. He tried so hard to get me up front, but there wasn't space.' I was like, look at me, I'm fit to be tied right now."

She gave herself a little pep talk. "Okay, Michele, you can either be angry and stamp your feet, or you can decide to work this through." She took out her journal and began writing.

Slowly, she said, her anger faded, allowing her to reframe. "I realized how ridiculous I sounded. I would've never seen this before. Now I realize these disturbances are opportunities for me to breath, look at it, and choose a different way to see it."

5. Take Back Your Projections

You will learn what you are by what you've projected
onto others and therefore believe that they are.
—*A COURSE IN MIRACLES*

You came into this world as a pure and innocent being. Go ahead and glance at one of your baby pictures if you find that hard to believe. Over time, however, you learn what is acceptable about you and what is not. You believed that the unacceptable part made you so unlovable and unworthy that if people knew the truth, they'd instantly hate or reject you. So you disowned those unacceptable parts by pushing them into your subconscious and pretended they're not who you are.

What you don't realize is that these aspects must somehow find expression, so you unconsciously project those repressed parts onto other people, organizations, or the world enabling you to get rid of them in you. As a result, you keep seeing "out there" whatever you're afraid to face in yourself.

To reframe an upset, explore how that person or situation is mirroring a shadow aspect in you, a part that needs your love and acceptance, a part that is coming up to be healed.

I keep several framed photos of me as a baby and toddler displayed in my room. I call it my Altar of Truth. One I especially love is me at about age two, sitting in a tiny chair in front of a mirror. I'm leaning forward kissing my reflection. When I'm feeling down about myself, I look at that beautiful child, making it much easier to unconditionally love myself, just as I am.

Your projections, however, include not just what you dislike about yourself, but all your wonderful gifts that you believe are too powerful, too glorious, too lovable, and too magnificent, so you project them onto others and feel envy or jealousy, admiration or attraction. Everyone is your mirror. As I wrote in my first book, Prince Charming is simply a projection of the powerful, responsible part you refuse to acknowledge in yourself. When you take back your projections and shift to recognition, you'll come to own the truth of who you *really* are.

"Our most hated, feared, or shamed qualities are the ones that hold the key to living the life of our dreams," wrote Debbie Ford in her powerful book *The Dark Side of the Light Chasers.*[6]

When you accept and own of all parts of you that you once judged as unacceptable, you'll discover tremendous gifts, strengths, and talents in your shadows. It's not about being "perfect." It's about discovering how that aspect can serve you.

6. Remember Your Intention

Choose your intention carefully and then
practice holding your consciousness to it, so it
becomes the guiding light in your life.
—ROGER DELANO HINKINS

You're reading this book for a reason, right? There's something you *really* want to accomplish—in fact, you wrote it down in the Introduction and again in Chapters 3 and 4. Right now, go back and read it again (page 77). Focusing on your intention stimulates the brain to seek opportunities to reach it. Particularly if your intention is important to you, if you believe achieving it will undeniably improve your life, you can use your intention as a framework and an inspiration for reframing.

Otherwise, as Dr. Michael Merzenich, an award-winning pioneer in brain plasticity research, wrote in his book *Soft-Wired*: "If it doesn't matter to you, and if you don't have to try to succeed, nothing much will change in your brain."[7]

Even though my Ego's quieted down significantly after a few sessions of EMDR, every so often, while working on this book, it stridently informs me that I write like sh*t. Instead of taking its words to heart, as I used to, I now reframe by responding, "Thank you for sharing, but I'm not going to listen. Just because I have a sh**ty draft doesn't mean I'm a sh**ty writer. I believe my Soul inspired me to write this because there may be one woman out there who needs to read this." When my nasty Ego continues its tirade, I shift my attention to that one person whose life may considerably improve because of my book.

7. Say a Prayer

The function of prayer is not to influence God, but rather to change the nature of the one who prays.
—SØREN KIERKEGAARD

Asking for help from your Higher Power is always a good idea. But let me share with you one particular prayer that I have hanging in my office. It's called "The OTHER Serenity Prayer" I didn't know the author until I quoted this prayer in a blog and Eleanor Brownn, an inspirational writer in Southern California, emailed to tell me she wrote it. I thanked her profusely. Repeating the words, sometimes aloud, always softens me up, opens my heart and allows me to reframe.

> *God, grant me the serenity to stop beating myself up*
> *for not doing things perfectly,*
> *the courage to forgive myself because I am working*
> *on doing better,*
> *and the wisdom to know You already love me just*
> *the way I am.*[8]

7

STEP #3: RESPOND DIFFERENTLY

Respond—verb—to react in response
Differently—adverb—in a different manner
—MERRIAM-WEBSTER DICTIONARY

ENTERING THE CAVE

Wanderer, There is no path. You lay the path by walking.
—ANTONIO MACHADO

The famed mythologist Joseph Campbell once said, "The cave you fear to enter holds the treasure that you seek." I lean on those words every time I commit to achieving that which I deeply desire. I've learned by now that what I *really* want is usually hidden in a dark and frightening cave.

I remember a woman, at a retreat, complaining, "I always let fear stop me."

"That is the definition of playing small," I told her. Admittedly, taking the third step by *Responding Differently* is not for the faint of heart. But even the most daring can be daunted.

A few years ago, I hired a highly respected, high-priced business coach, Ali Brown, to help me grow my business. I'd been steadily making six figures. I was ready to kick it up to seven. She encouraged me to raise my fees for my live retreats, charging way more than I felt comfortable with. I've raised my prices before, many times. Heck, I've written books on the topic. And I've personally coached thousands of women to do the same. Yet as I followed my own advice, I watched my anxiety meter shoot through the roof. I was filled with dread, like I'd be punished for doing something I shouldn't or be humiliated when no one signed up and my business went belly-up. Of course, I knew better. Neither came to pass. I had an incredibly profitable year, doing work I dearly loved. Yet even for me, going to that next level in earnings meant entering an unfamiliar cave, and it was undeniably scary.

This is what the third step—*Respond Differently*—calls you to do. It may be the most challenging of the three steps. As Jeffrey Schwartz noted, "You have to expend the effort and energy to recruit different brain pathways and make different choices each time you are confronted with the urge to follow your old ways."[1]

Refusing to follow your old ways is what will ultimately demolish the unwanted circuitry. Step #3 works like a wrecking ball aimed directly at the current connections between neurons. Another way to look at this step: Think of the scene in *The Wizard of Oz* when Dorothy, in a moment of terror, throws water on the wicked witch who suddenly screams, "I'm melting! I'm melting!"

The moment you respond differently, despite your trepidation, that nefarious neural network will begin to fade as a healthier one takes its place. If only it was as easy as flinging a bucket of water in the air, though.

The third step is an act of defiance—defiance against the intense attraction of the old neuropathways and the Ego's ruthless propaganda that you're powerless and incapable of change, so why bother. When you respond differently, you embark on the path marked *"Enter at Your Own Risk!"*

As you head toward the seemingly sinister cave in search of your treasure, I imagine your Ego looking like the ominous figure in Edward Munch's painting *The Scream*—eyes wide open in terror, clutching the sides of its face as it desperately warns you of the dangers ahead—rejection, disapproval, failure . . . oh my! Any attempt to enter will be met with ear-splitting shrieks: *"No!* Don't do it! Things won't go well! The results will be ugly! You'll be sorry!"

TAKE TWO STEPS BEFORE STRETCHING

We cannot change what we refuse to confront.
—ANONYMOUS

I've actually written about this step, referring to it as the Stretch, in my previous books. I learned from my interviews with highly successful women that their willingness to stretch beyond what felt comfortable to what seemed impossible was, by far, the leading factor in their stellar success—financially and professionally.

I often ask underearners, "When's the last time you did something you were scared to do?" They'd scratch their heads and struggle to recall an example. When I ask high earners the same question, they laugh and say, "All the time. It's a way of life." I even dubbed their typical response the *High Earners Slogan*: "If it's not illegal or immoral, I just say yes."

In fact, after one of those conversations, ages ago, I grabbed a piece of paper and wrote, in red crayon: *Do What You Fear. That's How You Succeed.* I framed it and put it on a table across from my desk where it still stands today. Looking at it now, I think I need to add: *But Don't Forget to Rewire.*

As I reflect on those interviews, I recall how every one of these courageous confident women initially struggled with fear, self-doubt, and feeling like a fraud, but didn't let it stop them. They inspired me to do the same. What's strikes me now is how many still felt like a fraud long after their careers were flourishing.

I remember reading that award-winning Maya Angelou, after publishing her eleventh book, thought to herself: "Uh-oh, they're going to find out now. I've run a game on everybody."[2]

In neuroscience, I found a possible explanation as to why imposter syndrome is epidemic among women, even the most successful ones. Despite their achievements, these women never rewired their old belief system. They didn't prepare themselves mentally as they pushed themselves physically. Because they hadn't changed their mindset, their brains continued to see only the past. Their self-image hadn't caught up with their successes. Their old neuropathways still dictated their current perceptions.

Successfully rewiring for wealth, well-being, or anything else necessitates that before you focus on changing your behavior, you must deal with the causes of that behavior—your thoughts and beliefs.

Trying to respond differently (Step #3) without recognizing (Step #1) and reframing (Step #2) is tantamount to running a marathon without first getting into shape. It's doubtful you'll get very far. And, even if you're driven to go the distance, you'll find little joy, but lots of discomfort, in your journey. The previous two steps in The Rewire Response provide the mental training needed to successfully and thoroughly complete this transformational process.

To illustrate how this step works, let me tell you the story of a woman who responded differently in the face of sometimes debilitating fear and anxiety. You'll learn from her a series of helpful tips for taming your anxiety and get a taste of the treasures you'll unearth as a result of your efforts. I'm reminded of something Joseph Jaworski says we must do in one of my favorite books, *Synchronicity*: "Listen to what's wanting to emerge. Then have the courage to do what's required." To me, those words neatly sum up the spirit of this third step.

TRACY'S STORY: SEVEN TIPS FOR TAMING ANXIETY AND CULTIVATING COURAGE

I will not use my own past learning as light to guide me now.
—A COURSE IN MIRACLES

Tracy Benson is an articulate and astute businesswoman who kept unwittingly sabotaging the consulting firm she founded. The company would be flying high, piling up profits, then suddenly take a dive into significant debt. When the debt reached six figures, she'd finally step on the brakes, figure out a plan to pay it off, work on it for years, return to stability until it happened all over again.

The month Tracy joined my Rewire Mentorship Program, she discovered she had Lyme disease, a debilitating tick-borne illness. Though she'd been suffering the painful symptoms for over five years, she took great pride in the fact that no one—not friends, family, colleagues, clients—ever knew she was sick.

I suspected there was a connection between her penchant for secrecy and her pattern of recurring debt. As a rule, whatever is going on with money is playing out in other areas of life as well.

"Why did you ignore your symptoms, keeping them a secret for so long?" I asked.

"In my family," she replied matter-of-factly, "I was always expected to show up as independent, strong, able to handle anything, take care of everyone else. There was absolutely no room for showing any vulnerability. If I spoke my truth, I'd be yelled at and called selfish."

"This is the neuropathway we have to weaken," I told her, "the one that says, 'Don't show who I *really* am, that I'm in financial trouble or actually sick. It's dangerous to speak your truth.'"

As Tracy connected the dots, she didn't like what she saw. "At the height of my success, I was doing stupid ass things to take care of my team while I was putting my own self into debt," she realized. "Our clients, big companies like GE, had payment terms of 90 days. Yet I put in contracts with every one of my employees and contractors that they would always be paid in 30 days."

She'd cover the cash shortage with a line of credit from the bank. "I was taking care of others but killing myself."

She paused, as if mulling over this new insight. "When you're in those patterns that don't make sense, you're in it so deep that you don't know they don't make sense." Amen to that!

Recognizing how her brain had been wired, she reframed her situation as a perfect opportunity to start doing things differently.

Tip #1 for Taming Anxiety: Breathe

"Keep taking deep breaths," I instruct clients as they're dipping their toes into unfamiliar waters.

Deep breathing (and yawning) reduces stress, sends oxygen to the brain, activates the calming parasympathetic nervous system, and increases dopamine (a neurotransmitter that effects pleasure and motivation). As your anxiety wanes, you'll find your courage increases.

"I know the next piece is finding the courage to come out of hiding," she declared as she took a deep breath.

Tip #2 for Taming Anxiety: Enter the Cave

Though it feels counterintuitive, acting in spite of fear will calm your nerves as you fail to detect any signs of danger, allowing the logical brain to leap back into operation, helping you make healthier decisions. Avoidance, on the other hand, always activates the limbic system's fear-seeking sensor, heightening anxiety.

Despite her apprehension, Tracy gradually began telling friends, then clients, about her illness. She tentatively, then eagerly, opened up on Facebook, sharing her story.

Tip #3 for Taming Anxiety: Positive Self-Talk

One day, she found herself being "crabby" to a colleague. But instead of making herself wrong or trying to conceal her feelings, she proudly acknowledged her progress. "I am in a terrible mood," Tracy observed. "It actually made me laugh because I saw I wasn't hiding, and it felt extremely liberating."

"What you say to yourself can change the way you see yourself," according to a study reported in the *New York Times*.[3] It's important, when in the throes of fear, to speak to yourself as if you're a loving parent or an encouraging friend, saying things like, "You can do this. You'll be great." And after you take action, congratulate yourself, regardless of the results: "You did it. You're not hiding anymore. I'm so proud of you."

Tip #4 for Taming Anxiety: Use Anger to Fuel You

After five years of being misdiagnosed, Tracy grew outraged by how little the medical community knew about Lyme disease. "I'm really pissed at how misunderstood it is," she fumed as she added, "Doctors kept telling me it was all in my head." So she used the gravity of the disease to fuel her into action rather than letting it eat her up inside. Repressed anger is toxic and immobilizing. But expressed anger can be galvanizing.

As she readily admits, "My frustration allowed me to let go of my old image of invincibility and to come out of hiding, tell my story, and advocate for others."

Tip #5 for Taming Anxiety: Make It Meaningful

Tracy launched a blog where she talked about coping with her symptoms and posted articles about Lyme disease on social media.

"I have a gift with words. I can explain things to people," declared Tracy, a communication expert. "I feel driven to inform and advocate for people who may be suffering."

Tracy's strong desire to help others through difficult times, which had long been her life's purpose, took precedence over her urge to keep hiding. She used her unwanted circumstances as the impetus to walk through fear and find meaning in her misery.

Tip #6 for Taming Anxiety: Remind Yourself Often—on the Other Side of Fear Lies Your Power

It's tempting to focus on how frightening it is to respond differently and all the bad things that could happen. But what if you entertained the possibility that you could be rewarded? Tracy took her biggest stretch when she joined a women's business group and was the first to volunteer for "30 minutes in the hot seat" in front of a small online gathering of perfect strangers.

"If I'm really going to show who I am, here's a scripted opportunity to do it," she told me. "It was a pretty remarkable experience."

Tracy was indeed rewarded. "I learned that the risks of putting myself out there and taking care of me are not what I thought they were," she exclaimed. "I always felt I would lose everyone's approval and acceptance if I was open about my struggles. But when the 30 minutes were up and the moderator said anyone who wants to can hang up, no one did. We continued the discussion for another 10 minutes. I felt so powerful."

Tip #7 for Taming Anxiety: Don't Wait Till It's Too Late

Studies have shown that the biggest regret people have on their deathbed is not what they did, but *what they didn't do.* If for no other reason, make yourself respond differently so you don't leave this world with your song still unsung or your gifts left unwrapped. One of my favorite country artists, Kris Kristofferson, sings a line, in a tune he wrote, that would make a helpful mantra: "I'd rather be sorry for something I did than for something I didn't do."

Before we move on, I'd like you to do this next exercise. You'll find it'll go a long way in helping you defuse your fear.

● Rewire in Action ●

RECALLING A RISK

Think of a risk you took in the past that had a positive outcome and you're particularly proud of.

Risk you're proud of: _____

_____

What you did to accomplish it: _____

_____

Now review your experience and jot down some additional notes about it.

Why you did it: _____

_____

What helped you succeed: _____

_____

What got in the way: _____

_____

How you overcame fear and resistance: _____

_____

Did you notice that the fear of doing was worse than the actual doing? How did you feel afterward—more confident, more powerful, stronger? How can you apply these realizations to a current challenge requiring you to respond differently?

_____

_____

AM I REALLY REWIRING?

*Any attempt to master fear is useless. The true
resolution rests entirely on mastery through love.*
—*A COURSE IN MIRACLES*

Here's the litmus test to tell if you're actually integrating the three steps, not just going through the motions: *You won't feel like yourself.* You'll look in the mirror and say, "Who is this person?" And you'll find yourself thinking, "This is not me." A part of you will be chomping at the bit to return to "normal."[4]

"The instant we don't feel like our old self," Joe Dispenza wrote in *Breaking the Habit of Being Yourself,* "that's the moment we know we're changing."[5]

Yes, you'll be tempted to flip back to the familiar. But the more you repeat the new responses, the easier it will get and the more normal you will feel. But what happens when you get stuck—when you can't seem to recognize, reframe, or respond differently, or when you feel the old neuropathways stubbornly refuse to relinquish control no matter how hard you try?

This answer lies in Part III: Hardwiring. Throughout the next three chapters, you'll be given a set of Power Tools with specific instructions for using them to stay the course and quell the demons holding you hostage. The Power Tools are:

1. **Resistance work.** How to take the path of *most* resistance (Chapter 8).
2. **Reparenting.** How to heal your inner child who's likely running the show (Chapter 9).
3. **Repetition.** How to keep repeating the new behaviors until a habit is formed (Chapter 10).

PART III

Hardwiring

Courage is being scared to death and saddling up anyway.
—JOHN WAYNE

8

POWER TOOL #1: RESISTANCE WORK

Most of us have two lives. The life we live, and the unlived life within us. Between the two stands Resistance.
—STEVEN PRESSFIELD

NO, NOT YET!

Change is never painful, only the resistance to change is painful.
—BUDDHA

You know the feeling. You're about to make a big change and do things differently. Let's say, for example, you decide to get out of debt and start building wealth. You schedule a meeting with a credit counselor, download a budgeting app, sign up for a financial class, and buy a book on investing. Off you go . . . when suddenly, you run smack dab into *Resistance*.

It may be a voice in your head, a feeling in your gut, or just a knee-jerk reaction, but your brain's message is unmistakably clear: *I don't want to do this! And you can't make me!* You forget the appointment, ignore the app, lose interest in the book, and sit through class but nothing registers. Eventually you quit trying.

I can't help but think of a cartoon I saw years ago: a saint stands with his arms outstretched, his gaze toward heaven, the caption reads: "God, give me chastity . . . but not yet."

This is exactly what resistance feels like. *You say you want to create wealth, and you really do . . . but . . . well . . . maybe not right now.* This feeling may be more insistent for some than for others. But you will undoubtedly experience a certain degree of resistance the moment you respond differently than you have in the past.

I've always compared wealth building to weight loss. We all know how to lose weight. Eat less and exercise more. Simple, right? Yet there's a billion-dollar diet industry devoted to helping people stay on track. Same with wealth building. There are only three things you need do—spend less, save more, and invest wisely. But, like dieting, people just can't seem to stick to these steps despite their steadfast desire to do so.

Resistance kicks in the moment you step out of your comfort zone and enter the Gap, the space between where you are now and where you want to be. The Gap is extremely uncomfortable, filled with tension. Your prevailing beliefs collide with your budding desires.

Your frightened Ego is trying its best to bring you back where you belong, while entrenched neuropathways are valiantly fighting for their very life. After all, the third step in the rewire process—Respond Differently—is like kryptonite to existing cognitive circuits. Each time you respond differently, you're sprouting and strengthening new neuropathways while sounding the death knell to old ones.

As a coach, the biggest challenge I have is getting clients past their resistance. Until that happens, they are neither receptive to learning nor willing to change. Yet I've rarely seen this topic addressed in financial courses or books. Until right now.

WHAT IS RESISTANCE?

Two souls, alas, are housed within my breast /
And each will wrestle for the mastery there.
—JOHANN WOLFGANG VON GOETHE

There's a story of two caterpillars who spy a butterfly overhead. One looks up longingly. The other snorts, "You'll never get me in that contraption." Resistance, like those caterpillars, is *a psychological reaction to an internal conflict.* Part of you wants to fly (your Soul). Another part doesn't (your Ego). Or to put it more scientifically, your rational brain, the cerebral cortex, is duking it out with your amygdala, or fear center, lodged in the limbic system. As long as those parts continue to butt heads, you'll remain hopelessly deadlocked.

Psychologists use the term *cognitive dissonance* to describe this phenomenon of holding two conflicting beliefs at the same time. This internal conflict gives rise to enormous anxiety, prompting you to lapse into mind-numbing defense mechanisms like denial, repression, or passive-aggressive behavior. Unless you understand this psychological condition, the effects can be quite disconcerting and destabilizing.

Cognitive dissonance also explains why a popular spiritual principle doesn't always work. There's a lot of talk these days about the *Law of Attraction*, which says *you attract whatever you want into your life through your ability to feel good, think positive, and focus only on the desired outcome.* But what's rarely mentioned is the *Law of Congruence*, which says *you get what you want, not what you ask for.* How do you know what you want? Look around at what you've attracted.

"What you ask for, you receive. But this refers to prayers of the heart, not the words you use in praying," explains *A Course in Miracles.* You may say you want wealth, but if you believe money is the root of all evil or rich people are greedy or if you have more, others will have less, then wealth isn't what you *really* want. What you *really* want is to stay safe, be liked, and be seen as a good person.

A big part of training your mind to rewire your brain is discerning between what your Ego *says* you want and what your Soul truly, genuinely, deeply desires, then making a conscious choice between the two. Resistance work is, in essence, conflict resolution.

Michele Phillips—a financially successful corporate trainer, author, and executive coach we met earlier—joined my program just as she moved to a very chic and well-heeled community, South Hampton, outside New York City. Surrounded by excessive wealth, she felt entirely out of place. When she started describing "all those people with money," I immediately interrupted her.

"Why are you talking as if there's two separate groups of people—those with money and you?"

I clearly hit a nerve. "Wait!" she said, somewhat startled. "I'm creating the separation based on my wiring, my old belief system. Aren't I?"

Michele saw herself as an outsider in her new surroundings because of her parents' negative attitude toward the affluent. Her poverty consciousness was clashing with her current reality: she and her husband, both financially well-off, were a long way away from scarcity.

"I got so off track," she admitted. "Now I just need to bridge this belief to rewire. My life is not matching who I think I am, but I can shift it. I can rewire it." And she did. When I talked to her later, she told me, "I've made so many good friends. I feel totally at home here."

THE TRUTH ABOUT RESISTANCE

Resistance is the first step to change.
—LOUISE HAY

Here's what I want you to keep in mind. Resistance is *not* bad, nor does it mean something's wrong. Resistance is a normal, natural, inevitable reaction to change. In fact, *resistance is good*. It's a sign you're rewiring.

You see, resistance isn't the problem, it's a symptom of something deeper. Let's take a moment to dissect this predictable opposition to change. All resistance comes from fear. At the core of all fear is a belief. At the root of each belief is a decision you made. A decision you came to usually early in life that has little to do with reality, is rarely true, and lies buried below your consciousness. Yet, like an invisible puppeteer pulling your strings, those unconscious decisions will control your behavior until you draw back the curtain and expose the truth.

So, let's do an exercise called Digging Deeper to help you shed light on unconscious decisions you believe to be true. Remember, you must first see them to reframe them.

Rewire in Action

DIGGING DEEPER

Complete the following sentences with the first word (or words) that come to mind. Don't censor what you get or look for the "right" answer. Let yourself go with your very first response. And do it quickly. You can always make changes later.

1. My father felt investing was _____

   _____

2. My mother felt investing was _____

   _____

3. In my family, money caused _____

   _____

4. My earliest memory of money is _____

   _____

5. Wealthy people are _____

   _____

6. My biggest fear of investing is _____

_____

7. I wish I had more money but _____

_____

8. My friends feel wealth is _____

_____

9. Investing equals _____

_____

10. I'd love to be wealthy but _____

_____

How did it feel to fill out these statements? Were there any surprises or responses that created new awareness? Did you discover anything that could be influencing your relationship with investing or wealth building today? Make some quick notes in the space below. If nothing came up, that's OK. Your mind is processing the information. It's quite common for insights to pop up in the middle of the night or as you're driving to work.

_____

_____

_____

_____

_____

_____

THIRTEEN SIGNS OF RESISTANCE

All changes, even the most longed for, have their melancholy:
for what we leave behind us is a part of ourselves: we
must die to one life before we can enter another.
—ANATOLE FRANCE

How do you know when you're in resistance? Obviously, whenever you feel stuck, unable to move forward. But be warned, resistance can be quite cunning, making it difficult to spot and easy to attribute to something else. Here are the 13 most common signs you're in resistance.

1. **You're too busy. ("I have no time.")**
2. **You procrastinate. ("I'll do it later.")**
3. **You're scared into inaction. ("But, what if . . . ?")**
4. **You defer decisions. ("You do it, you decide.")**
5. **You lose interest. ("This is boring, it's not my thing.")**
6. **You're forgetful. ("Oh, I meant to, but I forgot.")**
7. **You're disorganized. ("Where did I put that . . . ?")**
8. **You fog up, space out. ("What are you talking about?")**
9. **You feel paralyzed. ("I just can't think or get going.")**
10. **You find reasons not to act. ("I can't because . . .")**
11. **You're impatient. ("This is taking way too long.")**
12. **You keep taking classes but nothing changes. ("Oh look, another seminar I'll sign up for . . .")**
13. **You continually run into naysayers. (Others constantly say, "You can't do that" or "That's not possible." You're projecting your own fear onto others.)**

You may want to keep this list where you can easily access it. Whenever you're displaying one of these signs, realize you're in resistance. But, rest assured, resistance doesn't need to stop you, at least not for very long, if you know how to work with it. Once you identify resistance, you can start weakening it by employing the four stages of resistance work.

THE FOUR STAGES OF RESISTANCE WORK

Any change, even a change for the better, is always accompanied by drawbacks and discomforts.
—ARNOLD BENNETT

There's a natural tendency, when resistance strikes, to browbeat yourself mercilessly, bulldoze your way forward, or avoid the issue and abandon hope. None of these are helpful in the long run. What you ignore, you empower. What you resist, persists. What you hate, you become. Instead, when you recognize you're displaying any signs of resistance, remind yourself it's a positive sign that you're rewiring, then work with your resistance by engaging in these four stages:

1. **Honor your resistance by exploring it.**
2. **Pinpoint the conflict by reflecting on your past.**
3. **Proceed incrementally by taking on small, doable tasks.**
4. **Receive support by reaching out.**

Rewire in Action

WHERE AM I IN RESISTANCE?

Before we discuss how to work with resistance, in the space below write down where you are in resistance in your life right now. It need not be about money. It can be about anything.

Where you are experiencing resistance in your life right now?

_____

_____

_____

_____

Now that you know what you need to work on, it's time to learn what you can do to tackle resistance in your own life right now.

Stage 1: Honor Your Resistance by Exploring It

*When you experience resistance, you find the
lessons that you are meant to learn.*
—JON GORDON

I stumbled on this first stage of resistance a few years after my second divorce. I was ready to meet my PMFM ("Perfect Man for Me."). But the men I'd been attracting didn't fit the bill. So I hired a relationship coach. After each session, she'd give me homework, which I'd never do.

During what would be our last appointment, the words unexpectedly, but adamantly, flew out of my mouth: "Look, Janis, I'm in resistance. And I'm going to stay in resistance until I'm not in resistance anymore."

I hung up feeling great. It was actually a relief to honor my resistance by respecting my truth. I wasn't avoiding anything. Quite the opposite. I saw my refusal to do the homework as an opportunity to figure out what my resistance was trying to tell me—about my fears, beliefs, and early decisions. I proceeded to do some considerable soul searching by asking the questions in the exercise below and having an inquiry with my resistance.

● Rewire in Action ●

AN INQUIRY WITH RESISTANCE

You can explore your resistance by asking yourself the following questions and writing your responses below:

What am I afraid of? _____

_____

Why am I afraid? _____

_____

What belief is my resistance reflecting? _____

_____

What decision did I make as a result of my belief? _____

_____

(continued)

How is my past experience provoking my resistance? _____

_____

What is the payoff for staying where I am? _____

_____

After asking myself these questions, I discovered I harbored a mother lode of anger against men. Staying single, I realized, felt safer, less painful than being in a relationship. I wasn't surprised anger was the source of my resistance. In my experience, women in general hold a tremendous amount of unexpressed anger, though few realize it. I believe buried anger (along with unhealed trauma) is perhaps our biggest barrier to financial success. I see it with almost every woman I coach. I've seen it in myself through the years. Most of us don't like anger. It doesn't feel good. It's not feminine. It's not "nice." It's scary. Historically we've been groomed to repress our rage and thus worry that if we lift the lid, even a tiny bit, our wrath will suddenly erupt, engulfing us in a flood of hot lava.

The truth is, anger is a natural human emotion. Healthy when expressed in a timely manner. Toxic when bottled up.

"Holding onto anger," as Buddha wisely pointed out, "is like grasping a hot coal with the intent of throwing it at someone else; you are the one who gets burned."[1]

It takes a lot of energy to stifle emotions. Repressed anger clogs up your thinking, drains your creativity, and weighs you down like a concrete block. Released anger frees you and stimulates action.

In my determination to heal, I did an exercise I'd done in the past—writing an angry letter. I often have clients write angry letters. As one told me after she wrote hers: "At first it was scary. I felt so rageful. But I also felt a release that I'd never felt before."

I'm convinced that it's no coincidence that I met my husband shortly after I completed my letter.

Rewire in Action

ANGRY LETTER

If you suspect you may have some buried anger, I invite you to write an angry letter. Maybe to your parents or your ex-husband. Perhaps to yourself. Write it by hand, not on a computer. Start the letter with "Dear XX, I am so pissed at you . . ." (using whatever words feel right). Let yourself get into it, liberating your fury, your frustrations. Write until you're done.

Next fold up the letter and put it away for no more than three days.

Then take it out and reread it. Is there anything you want to add? If so, keep writing. Continue the process until you feel complete.

When you're finally finished, burn the letter, ritualistically. As it burns, say to your anger: "Thank you. You served me once. I no longer need you. I release you. You are free. I am free."

You'll know if you've sufficiently discharged your anger if, after you complete your angry letter, you can follow up with a letter of gratitude, acknowledging how those infuriating experiences have made you the incredible woman you are today. If you can't find the gift that experience has given you, you've still got more anger to release.

What if you've done anger releasing exercises ad nauseum, and damn it, you're still angry? Ask yourself: What is my payoff for holding onto

(continued)

anger? Why don't I want to let it go? Believe me, the anger is giving you something. Often, it's a false sense of power, invulnerability, or autonomy. But I promise, the so-called benefits are nothing compared to the lightness you'll feel once your anger's lifted.

Stage 2: Pinpoint the Conflict by Reflecting on the Past

If I get stuck in who I am now, I will never
blossom into who I might yet become. I need
to practice the gentle art of letting go.
—SAM KEEN

Melissa, a medical editor, signed up for coaching hoping to increase her savings, understand her investments, and find a new career. Freshly out of debt for the second time, she vowed, "It will never happen again."

Yet she was reluctant to look at her financial statements ("I'm afraid what I'll see") or explore another career ("I can't possibly do something new. I don't know enough."). We were both frustrated by her procrastination.

"I feel like a cat hanging by its claws," she said, vividly describing how exasperating resistance can be.

"What was life like for you as a child?" I asked, hoping to pinpoint her internal conflict. Resistance often indicates a discord between one's early conditioning and one's authentic self.

"My parents constantly ridiculed me," she recalled. "They called my ideas dumb, stupid, ridiculous. I always felt on edge, anxious, fearful. It had a life-death feel to it."

As Melissa rummaged around her past, she had a stunning revelation. "I just realized I'm deathly afraid of making mistakes because of all the ridicule I suffered growing up." She clearly saw that the messages she received as a child were "in a great war" with her Soul's urges. Melissa, like many intelligent women who have inexorable money issues, desperately needed to individuate from her parents.

Individuation is a developmental phase when a child separates from her family of origin, a phase many adults, particularly women, have yet to complete. Individuation insists that you take from your upbringing what serves you and discard what doesn't, carefully distinguishing what's true *for you* from what's been artificially imposed. This means finding the strength to let go of what no longer fits—all the *shoulds*, *oughts*, and *musts*—that get in the way of who you genuinely are and actually could be.

Failure to individuate when young tends to surface later on as an inexplicable refusal to move forward, not just with money but in other areas of life as well.

Melissa began the individuation process with a seemingly simple but surprisingly painful act. She unfriended her family on Facebook.

"It's amazing how difficult it was to block my family. I feel so alone, like I'm an orphan. Like there's a child in me yearning for the love I never had."

"That is exactly what individuation feels like," I assured her. "It's sad. You need to grieve. But it's ultimately freeing."

Unfriending her family was a turning point for Melissa. Her ability to set firm boundaries boosted her confidence, ignited her motivation to change, and noticeably diminished her resistance.

I began giving Melissa small assignments.

Stage 3: Proceed Incrementally by Taking on Small, Doable Tasks

The mind can deliver incremental gains, not quantum leaps.
—ALEX HUTCHINSON

If you've ever worked out in a gym, you know that you build muscles by lifting progressively heavier weights. It's aptly called *resistance training*. You don't start off doing a chest press with a 100-pound barbell. Instead, you start with two, maybe five pounds and slowly work your way up. It's the same with building financial muscles. You start with easy activities, like simply skimming *Money* magazine or scrolling though Investopedia.com. Gradually, you let those steps get a little bit harder, like reading a whole article or taking an online class.

I had Melissa track her spending, which she initially resisted, fearful of what she'd find. "The goal here is not to eliminate fear. Because you can't," I informed her. "The goal is to act in spite of it."

She began writing down all her purchases. "It was eye opening," she exclaimed. "I found myself resisting but knew I had to. It was *really* hard during Christmas, but I did it. I wanted to buy gifts for clients. I baked cookies instead."

As she went through her monthly expenses and income, another assignment, she was delightfully surprised. "I'm doing quite well," she said, with tears of relief. "I was in debt for so long. My family has been too. This is not a place I ever thought I'd be."

When I asked what she attributed her success to, she replied, "I learned that small incremental changes add up a lot faster than you think they do. It's the consistency."

During this period, Melissa fell in love. "Bob is everything I had on my list."

That gave me an idea for addressing her work issues. "Why don't you make a list of everything you want in a career just like you did with a boyfriend?" I assigned her an exercise I relied on, years ago, when I was a career counselor—the Career Finder.

Rewire in Action

THE CAREER FINDER

Take a piece of paper and divide it into 3 columns.

Next, divide your age into thirds and write each third at the top of a separate column. If you're 30, the first column would be 1–10; the second would be 10–20; and the third, 20–30.

Then think back to achievements you had in each period when you felt powerful, important, skilled, and capable.

Recall something you did that went really well, that you felt extremely proud of, and that made you very happy—anything from learning to tie your shoes, to winning a sailboat race, to writing a story that made someone laugh.

Try to find at least three experiences within each age group. And write them in the appropriate column, leaving a lot of space between each achievement.

Then, alongside each achievement, describe in a few sentences what you did, the skills you used, the interests you displayed, the environments surrounding you.

Do you see any patterns? Pay particular attention to what brought you the most gladness, the things you did really well and enjoyed doing so much that you sometimes take them for granted.

Jot down what you discovered.

As Melissa described each of her most memorable and joyful accomplishments, we made a list of the common themes: touching people deeply; encouraging others; being a good listener; emotional honesty; creating safe space for people to be vulnerable. When I suggested the pattern pointed to psychotherapy or coaching, she was overjoyed.

"For the last 20 years I've thought of being a therapist," she exclaimed. "I'm in a good place now to do it. It's time."

Stage 4: Receive Support by Reaching Out

We don't heal in isolation, but in community.
—S. KELLEY HARRELL

"I've always known that I wanted to work with people around psychology," Melissa recalled, admitting she didn't have the courage to go for it. All that changed when she began reaching out for support.

"You gave me so much encouragement to explore coaching. And Bob has been totally supportive. I also got positive feedback from my therapist, who loved the idea of me coaching, and so did my friends."

Support is especially critical for women. We are relationship oriented, far more than men. We need people we trust to have our backs, hold us accountable, push us when things gets tough, or high-five us when we finally succeed. Rewiring specifically, and success in general, is not meant and should never be a solo journey, especially when you're in the Gap, not quite where you want to be.

I also had her reach out to her financial advisor. At first she was reluctant. But when she contacted him, she realized, as with everything she'd been doing, what was initially frightening was becoming progressively less scary and actually enjoyable.

"He was so excited I called him," she reported back. "He helped get me on their website where all my information is. We're going to dig deeper into my funds. I know how much I need to retire with $1 million. It feels so doable."

She was on fire now. "I figured out my net worth. It's higher than I thought. I got on the Morningstar website and took classes to learn about stocks."

This was our last session. Two years later, when I interviewed her for this book, Melissa's resistance was a distant memory. She told me she'd moved in with her boyfriend, re-friended her family on Facebook, and was about to become a certified coach.

As for finances, she observed, "I don't remember the last time I thought, 'Oh my God, one small slip and I'm a bag lady on the streets.' Those thoughts don't come anymore." she exclaimed. "I had to reach out and touch the monster, the monster being the money. With my advisor's help, the more I looked at it, the easier it became. I still talk to him all the time. I'm so much more relaxed, knowing my situation."

Below is an exercise that will give you get a quick snapshot of your support system. Most women find this very illuminating, often realizing their lack of support was the missing link in their efforts to achieve financial self-efficacy.

● Rewire in Action ●

SACRED WEALTH CIRCLE

The circle below is your Sacred Wealth Circle. Inside the circle, list the names of people you can talk to about wealth building and personal growth. Outside the circle, list those in your life who aren't interested in the topic or may frown upon your efforts.

What do you notice? Were there more names outside your circle than inside? Would you like to add people to your inner circle? You can never get enough support.

However, you must honor the boundaries of this Sacred Circle. Don't let anyone inside your circle who doesn't respect or endorse your effort. No pessimists, naysayers, or worrywarts allowed. Otherwise, it's too easy to succumb to the siren call of the hardwired neuropathway.

There are many ways to find support.

Find a group. Take a class, join an existing financial group, or form one yourself—say, a book club, a study group, or an investment club. Researchers from Emory University found that "the pleasure and reward centers of a woman's brain light up if they can work towards their financial goals in collaboration with other women."

Find a partner. Get a friend, fellow student, colleague, or family member to check in with regularly, share what you've accomplished (or didn't), and commit to what you'll do next. Once during a Rewire group call, a woman announced she'd just started using a budgeting app called YNAB.com (You Need A Budget) and was wanting help. Another woman on the call who was also new to the app spoke up immediately. "I'd love to be your partner," she volunteered. The two exchanged email addresses and agreed to contact each other weekly to report their progress, ask questions, and offer suggestions.

Reach out to professionals. In my research with successful women, the ones with the highest net worth didn't necessarily earn (or inherit) the most money, but each worked, at least at some point, with a team of experts, including an investment advisor, bookkeeper, accountant, and estate attorney.

Get a mentor. Whenever you meet someone who's financially savvy, enroll them as a mentor. This is what I did when I was trying to educate myself, and it worked like a charm. I didn't ask anyone outright to mentor

me. But I'd say: "If I have any questions about investing, could I ask you?" Or I'd invite them for coffee and
pick their brain. I found most people were eager to share
their knowledge and actually enjoyed knowing they
helped me.

HELP! I'M IRREPARABLY STUCK

*True resistance begins with people confronting pain . . .
and wanting to do something to change it.*
—bell hooks

What if, no matter what you do, you feel trapped in an
endless maze with no exit in sight? Persistent, unyielding
resistance is usually a sign that unresolved pain is weighing
you down, needing to be healed. The remedy can be found in
the next chapter, where you'll pick up another Power Tool—
Reparenting, a potent antidote for unremitting resistance.

9

POWER TOOL #2: REPARENTING

Until you heal the wounds of your past,
you will continue to bleed.
—IYLANA VANZANT

THE CHILD WITHIN

We often tend to ignore how much of
a child is still in all of us.
—ELISABETH KÜBLER-ROSS

When you look at yourself in the mirror, you see a grown woman staring back, right? But what you don't see in that mirror is the little girl who's very much alive inside you. A little girl whose needs probably weren't met growing up. A little girl who may have been abused, abandoned, rejected, traumatized, shamed, or mistreated in subtle ways. And this little girl is likely the reason your resistance won't let up. She's scared. She needs attention. But alas, you continue to ignore her.

"The inner child is real," writes psychologist and author Stephen A. Diamond in *Psychology Today*. "Not literally. Nor physically. But figuratively, metaphorically real. . . . a psychological or phenomenological reality, and an extraordinarily powerful one at that."[1]

Yet, he explains, very few are aware of their indwelling child-self with all its pain, trauma, fear, and anger.

Most adults think "they have successfully outgrown, jettisoned, and left this child—and its emotional baggage—long behind," Dr. Diamond explains. "But this is far from the truth. In fact, these so-called grown-ups or adults are unwittingly being constantly influenced or covertly controlled by this unconscious inner child."

The existence of the "inner child"—many credit Carl Jung with introducing the term—makes sense scientifically. During the first seven years of life, when you're most impressionable, stressful experiences are deeply and indelibly tattooed onto your developing brain. Whether you grew up in extensive poverty or even partial neglect, lived in a war-torn country or a strict religious cult, were bullied by your peers or belittled by your teachers, early life stress (ELS) causes a constant flow of cortisol to be released, adversely affecting your brain's growth.

"The functional capabilities of the mature brain develop throughout life, but the vast majority of critical structural and functional organization takes place in childhood," explains Bruce D. Perry, psychiatrist, author, and senior fellow of the Child Trauma Academy in Houston, Texas. "Simply stated, children reflect the world in which they are raised. If that world is characterized by threat, chaos, unpredictability, fear and trauma, the brain will reflect that."[2]

In a riveting, though heart-wrenching, *60 Minutes* episode on the subject, host Oprah Winfrey declared that we're facing "a twenty-first-century epidemic of childhood trauma."[3]

"If you're a child who's raised in a nurturing and well-cared-for environment," she opined during an interview with Dr. Perry, "You're more likely to have a well-wired brain."

The trauma specialist nodded his head, "Correct." But a child raised in a chaotic environment, he added, "will be wired differently. And typically, they have trouble functioning in the world in a way that makes them more vulnerable."

ELS is so widespread that our world is filled with the walking wounded. Consequently, as one of the leading figures in the field of family systems and relationships, John Bradshaw, said, "I believe that this neglected wounded inner child is the major source of human misery."

I couldn't agree more. In case you're wondering why I've devoted a whole chapter to reparenting in a book about wealth building, it's because, in my experience, it's often the wounded inner child acting out that causes otherwise intelligent, rational adults to create financial chaos.

A Course in Miracles explains that we're never upset for the reason we think. It's not the current difficulties that disturb us. It's how they trigger old memories, rip scabs off old wounds, catapult us back into a previous era. Whenever you're upset, the Course suggests, remind yourself, "I see only the past."

There's a wonderful metaphor commonly used to illustrate how this plays out. Imagine you are calmly driving the car while your inner child is safely strapped into her car seat in the back. Suddenly an angry driver screams at you. Your inner child, triggered by a threat that feels frightfully familiar, swiftly unbuckles her seat belt, leaps into the front seat, shoves you aside, and grabs the wheel, yelling, "I've got this!" Of course her feet can't touch the pedals, nor does she know how to drive. You, meanwhile, sit there stunned, not sure what just happened, but feeling totally out of control. Because you are: Out. Of. Control. Just as Sandra was when I met her.

SANDRA'S STORY

Your inner child is waiting for a genuine, heartfelt apology.
—YONG KANG CHAN

After years working as a bookkeeper, Sandra built a successful consulting business, helping entrepreneurs manage their company's money. She was financially savvy, earned a healthy income, and had plenty in savings, yet she was drowning in debt. She came to me for help, even though, on a practical level, she knew precisely what she needed to do.

"I know I should be using my debit card instead of credit cards," she admitted. "But it's crazy how much that scares me. I'm having a full-body freak-out moment right now just thinking about not using credit cards."

At first, I was taken aback, "I don't think I've ever had anyone as smart with money and as resistant as you," I told her bluntly. But as she reflected on her past, her behavior made more sense. She had suffered a very painful childhood. Her father abandoned her. A stepfather abused her. Her mother was emotionally absent. Escalating debt served as an expedient (albeit unconscious) diversion from the constant angst swirling inside her.

"I might suggest some trauma therapy if we don't make progress," I said.

"That definitely feels like something I've been avoiding," she chuckled.

"Why do you think you've been avoiding it?"

"The words that are coming up in my head are *That's just how we were raised, it wasn't any different than anybody else. You just suck it up.* I never thought of it as trauma. I always felt, *This is the life I was dealt. This is the best I can do.*"

"How does that feel to you now, as you say it?" I asked.

"I know that's not true. Its black-and-white thinking. But I seem to be hanging on to it."

My heart went out to her. Sandra's minimalizing her past experience and refusing to relinquish her credit cards were signs of a serious addiction.

"Addiction and other dangerous behaviors," explains author Lisa J Smith, in an article "Re-Parent Your Inner Child," "are some of the more serious issues attributed to allowing the inner child to make adult decisions."[4]

I urged her to go to Debtors Anonymous, a 12-step program designed especially for chronic spenders and compulsive debtors. I told her I attended DA meetings for years and explained how much it helped me. In our next session, Sandra told me she had checked out DA.

"Well, what did you think?" I asked, excited to know. She responded exactly like my ex did after he went to his first and only Gamblers Anonymous meeting.

"There's no way in hell I'm bad enough to go to DA. I'm not at all like those people."

What made me especially sad was that I knew how much she earnestly yearned to do for herself what she helped others do—take financial responsibility. Yet she clung to her debt like a life preserver, too scared to dive into the deep waters of healing.

"Most often, when we feel pain from a deep place within, it's our inner wounded child who's calling," Buddhist monk Thich Nhat Hanh said in his book *Reconciliation*. "Forgetting the pain results in more pain."[5]

Or as Dr. Diamond would add, "Remaining unconscious is what empowers the dissociated inner child to take possession of the personality at times, to overpower the will of the adult."

How do you know if your inner wounded child is acting out? Here's a list of clues.

• Rewire in Action •

SIGNS OF A WOUNDED INNER CHILD

These are some indicators that your inner child may be acting out. Check any that apply to you:

- [ ] You have weak boundaries or very rigid ones.
- [ ] You distrust yourself and/or others.
- [ ] You worry excessively.
- [ ] You're a people pleaser, craving approval.
- [ ] You're a high achiever, driven to be perfect, terrified to fail.
- [ ] You steer clear of strong emotions, yours or others.
- [ ] You're addiction prone.
- [ ] You're energized by conflict.
- [ ] You're dependent on routine, dislike change, avoid the unknown.
- [ ] You're afraid to state your opinion.
- [ ] You feel like something's very wrong with you.
- [ ] You're highly critical, of yourself and others.
- [ ] You stay too long in unhealthy situations.

HEALING YOUR WOUNDED INNER CHILD

*Many of us are guilty of not taking enough
time to dial into our inner child's voice.*

—KIM HA CAMPBELL

Healing your inner child takes courage, commitment, and motivation—all characteristics I've emphasized from the beginning of this book. Because the only way to heal old pain is to rewire the neuropathways sculpted by that pain. Thus we turn, again, to the three steps of The Rewire Response for nursing our young selves back to health.

- First you must *Recognize* that you're no longer in the driver's seat, but your life is now controlled by someone with the maturity level of a five-year-old.
- Then *Reframe* the situation. I particularly like Oprah's reframe on *60 Minutes*. Whenever you can't control your impulses, she advised viewers to ask themselves this question: *What's happened to me?* which she said "is a very different question than *What's wrong with me?*"
- Then *Respond Differently* by reparenting your wounded child.

Trauma specialists seem to agree that traumatized children need to be heard and seen by someone who they feel sincerely wants to help. This could be a trained therapist. But I've found that do-it-yourself-reparenting is extremely effective.

I help clients reparent themselves either by taking them through a guided visualization—which I've outlined below—or asking them to communicate, on their own, with their frightened inner child, at the age when she experienced trauma, taking time to listen to her pain. When the child feels heard, reassure her that, from now on, you'll protect her and she no longer needs to interfere in your life, firmly telling her, "I've got this. Get back in your seat. We're safe."

Rewire in Action

REPARENTING GUIDED VISUALIZATION

- Get comfortable.
- Close your eyes.
- Take three deep, cleansing breaths.
- Relax your whole body.
- Picture yourself in a safe place—real or imagined, indoors or out.
- In this safe place, bring in your little girl.
- Greet her in whatever way feels right.
- Find a place where you both can sit comfortably.
- Then ask her, "What was it like for you growing up?"
- Let her talk and you listen. Don't offer any advice. Be compassionate and loving.
- Assure her you love her and want her to feel safe and that, from now on, you will protect her.
- Insist you don't need her help anymore. You're going to keep her safe by making healthier decisions.
- Answer her questions and promise that you'll never leave her but will be there whenever she needs you.
- Before you leave, put her in the arms of a guardian angel who will love and heal her.
- Say goodbye, letting her know you'll be back.

As sociologist and author Martha Beck explained: "Caring for your inner child has a powerful and surprisingly quick result: Do it and the child heals."[6] Here are two examples of the power of caring for your inner child by doing the Reparenting Guided Visualization. In the first story, Amrita shows us how early trauma need not be physically violent, but can be subtle enough to be accepted as normal. Until she reparented her scared little girl, Amrita's brain virtually could not see the solution to her problem, even though it lay in plain sight. In the second story, Gretchen demonstrates how, despite horrific abuse, reparenting helped her overcome an addiction and find compassion for herself. As a result, she ended up taking daring actions that, until then, felt entirely too dangerous.

Let's learn from these brave and incredible women now.

AMRITA'S STORY

She held herself until the sobs of the child inside subsided entirely. I love you, she told herself. It will all be okay.
—H. RAVEN ROSE

Amrita had long avoided dealing with money or telling her husband about her mounting business debt. She joined my program because, she said, "I don't want to keep living in fear. When I get scared, something inside me kicks in and I freeze."

After several sessions, I began to suspect that it was her frightened little girl who kicked her adult self into freeze mode. I suggested we do an exercise to learn what her inner

child had to say. After I took Amrita through the guided visualization, I asked her to share her experience.

"She said her parents could be very fun at times, but other
times there were explosions of anger. She told me she learned
to be quiet and on her best behavior, especially after her father
left. Because she never knew when she'd see him next." She
paused briefly as if she was traveling back in time.

"He was so proud when he could show me off, in my
pretty dress. But when I was noisy or broke things or there
was too much chaos, he'd get very angry at me or at some-
body else in the room. I felt responsible."

"That's a big load for a little girl to carry," I remarked.

Amrita's immediate reaction was to defend her father, dismiss the damage. "It really wasn't a big deal," she argued.

Still, she agreed to do the visualization again at home.
"Next time, let her know how much you love her and you're
going to protect her by keeping her out of harm's way."

After repeating the exercise a number of times, she had
an epiphany. As if a blindfold had been ripped from her eyes,
Amrita looked at her accounts, and lo and behold, she saw
she had enough money to repay every penny of her debt. The
funds had been in the bank all along, but she hadn't been able
to see that until then.

Continually reassuring her inner child that she'd keep
her safe rewired Amrita's rational brain to start searching
for solutions instead of allowing her primitive brain to keep
repeating old patterns of self-protection.

"I couldn't find a way to pay the debt off even though the
amount I needed was always there in my personal savings,"
she said in amazement. "There were actually multiple ways I
could've paid it off much earlier. When I finally looked at the

numbers, because that was my homework, I saw how much was in each account. It was like a big door opened."

However, she admitted, she didn't want to walk through that door at first, actually pay off her debt. "It didn't feel good. It was hard to do."

"That's exactly what rewiring feels like," I assured her. "In fact, if it feels good in the beginning, you're way off track. If it feels like *Oh, no, this is wrong, it's not me*, you're definitely doing it right. Remember, your brain's old wiring exerts such an intense force, it takes tremendous vigilance at the outset not to get sucked back in."

On our final session, she excitedly told me: "I've started paying attention to all the other doors that have been opening and push myself to take action steps when I feel like I'm getting stuck." After doing the reparenting work, her little girl was now happily playing in the back seat, allowing Amrita to feel safe enough to have an honest conversation about money with her husband.

GRETCHEN'S STORY

The first step in the undoing is recognizing that you actively decided wrongly, but can actively decide otherwise . . . your part is merely to return your thinking to the point at which the error was made.
—*A COURSE IN MIRACLES*

Gretchen suffered from what I call SSA, *Serial Seminar Addiction*, often a sign of unhealed trauma. I see it all the time. People racing from one personal growth workshop to

163

another, giving them the illusion of working on themselves without doing the deeper healing required for change.

Stephen King summed up this syndrome perfectly when he said, "It is, after all, the dab of grit that seeps into an oyster's shell that makes the pearl, not pearl-making seminars with other oysters."[7]

Like all addictions, SSA is a means of avoiding the discomfort caused by "the dab of grit" instead of using it for personal transformation. Reparenting, however, provides a gentle but potent tool for quickly unearthing buried emotions.

When Gretchen joined my Rewire program, she was about to sign up for two more self-help classes. She'd been trapped for years in an abusive relationship with a man who supported her financially. In exchange, she managed his legal practice. With little money of her own, and even less confidence, she felt powerless to leave. I urged her not to take any more courses.

"Let's focus on rewiring your brain, instead of spreading your attention too thin," I said. "So you actually feel more powerful and make more constructive choices." She agreed.

In our sessions, Gretchen told me her father sexually abused her until he abandoned the family, leaving her and her mother in poverty. I began to suspect that her traumatized child was holding her hostage.

"Having someone take care of me financially felt nurturing," she declared. "I realize now I've been confusing my need to be loved by a man with being financially supported by a man."

I told her about reparenting, assigning it as homework. She had an immediate breakthrough.

"The process of reparenting myself gave me a lot of power," she told me later. "And it gave me a lot of compassion for myself. I think a lot of times it's easy for us to give that to other people, but not for ourselves so much."

Gretchen practiced reparenting every single night when she got into bed. "Sometimes I imagined a loving father tucking me in. He was the father I would've loved to have had, who made me feel safe and took care of me and held me in his big arms."

Other times, she saw herself as the parent. "I would picture the adult me picking her up and putting her in my lap and rocking her, telling her what I would tell my own children. She was loved. She wasn't alone. She hadn't done anything wrong."

Occasionally, she recalled, "It was my grandmother or some imagined benevolent beings who tucked me in at night, and made me feel safe."

After just a few months, she noticed a big difference. "Now, when I think of what my father did," she told me, "I'm not triggered in the same way. I don't feel the intense grief that I did. I don't know if I'm totally healed. There are still remnants from the trauma that occasionally surface, but they don't have the same sting. I'm aware of what happened to me, but it also makes me who I am, stronger for it."

I watched as Gretchen transformed from a helpless child into a proactive adult. She downloaded an app to track the hours she worked, figured out the going rate for an office manager, created a spreadsheet of her expenses, negotiated a living wage with her soon-to-be ex-partner. She told him she'd quit as his manager if he didn't pay her and also insisted he buy out her portion of the house and let her live there for free. After a lot of sometimes harsh back-and-forth discussion, he agreed.

"It was scary. He's a tough negotiator," she admitted. "But I got stronger through this process. I know I can trust myself." And her inner child could finally relax, knowing the adult Gretchen would take good care of her from now on. In fact, the last we talked, she had mustered up the nerve to tell him she was leaving.

Eight months later, her life had changed in ways she never dreamed possible. After she told him it was over, he was angry at first, but then begged her for another chance. She insisted he work on his issues with women, but even then, he'd have to really step up to win her back, but no guarantees. He immediately found a therapist and began meditating daily. To her amazement, his behavior and their living situation "drastically" improved.

MOVING ONWARD

We may never know exactly when or how this began, but if we acknowledge this little one, she will somehow know that we are listening to her.
—BONNIE BADENOCH

I doubt you'll find the topic of reparenting in any other books about money. But if you're experiencing prolonged financial distress, accompanied by unremitting resistance, that little girl who lives inside you is probably the culprit. She needs to feel safe and protected by you before she'll give you permission to move forward.

Reparenting doesn't require a big chunk of time. When I take clients through the guided visualization in this chapter, it only takes about 10 minutes, often less. You can even commune with your inner child, eyes open, while in line at the store, driving to work, or taking a shower. It's not the time you put in, but the degree of emotion you feel and the consistency with which you practice. Once you rewire your wounded inner child's brain—because that's what reparenting does—and become your own safe harbor, the next Power Tool will take considerably less effort to put into practice.

Before we move on, let me leave you with a few lines from a poem titled "My Child Within" by Kathleen Algoe that describes reparenting more poignantly than I ever could.

We hugged each other ever so tight
As feeling emerged of hurt and fright
It's okay, I sobbed, I love you so!
You are precious to me, I want you to know
My child, my child, you are safe today
You will not be abandoned, I'm here to stay
We laughed, we cried, it was a discovery
This warm loving child is my recovery.[8]

10

POWER TOOL #3: REPETITION

Almost without exception, those we know as masters are
zealots of practice, connoisseurs of the small incremental step.
—GEORGE LEONARD

ONLY REPETITION REWIRES

We are what we repeatedly do.
—ARISTOTLE

As you recall, the first two steps in The Rewire Response are
(1) *Recognize*—observe any negative or unhealthy thoughts or
feelings with curiosity, not criticism; and (2) *Reframe*—find
ways to perceive the situation differently. These steps have one
purpose: to transform your thinking, which will set you up
to successfully engage in the third step, *Respond Differently,*

not habitually. This third step, like an ignition key, actually switches on the rewiring process.

But without consciously and constantly employing the third Power Tool, *Repetition*, permanent rewiring is virtually impossible. *Responding differently*, not once, but over and over again, is what solidifies and locks in nascent neural connections. Research published in *Psychological Review* found that "forming good (and bad) habits depends more on how often you perform an action than on how much satisfaction you get from it."[1]

AN EXERCISE IN REPETITION

When people have the capacity to choose,
they have the ability to change.
—MADELEINE ALBRIGHT

Before we go any further, I'd like you to try an experiment. Bring both your hands together, interlacing your fingers. Now take your hands apart. Then clasp them together once more, interlacing your fingers. Again, take them apart. Do this a few more times. Together. Apart. Together. Apart. (C'mon, clasp and unclasp your hands a few times. I promise, I'm making a point here.)

What did you notice? If you're like most people, you probably folded your fingers into the same configuration each time, right?

This time, I want you to bring your hands back together, interlacing your fingers however feels comfortable. Now, let's rearrange your fingers. Take the top thumb and put it underneath the thumb under it. Bring the top index finger underneath the one below it. Do the same with the top middle finger, putting it underneath the finger beneath it. Continue with the ring finger, and finally the pinky.

How does that feel? Awkward? Uncomfortable? Weird? I'm guessing, when I ask you one last time to take them apart and bring them back together, you'll revert to the first formation that feels more "normal" because that's the way you've been wired. And challenging that wiring feels so uncomfortable, you instinctively revert to your old ways for temporary relief.

Now, imagine that your fingers, in this exercise, represent your thoughts, your feelings, or your actions. Your first attempts at thinking, feeling, or acting differently (like arranging your fingers differently) won't feel right. But rewiring requires you to respond differently again and again and again. Unless you keep exerting intense effort, the colossal force of the old circuitry will suck you back every time.

Responding differently is to an emerging neuropathway what weightlifting is to an atrophied muscle. You must do what you don't always feel like doing over and over again. The more often you repeat, the stronger the neuropathway (or muscle) grows. But it's so grueling at the outset that many give up. I guarantee, the more consistently you respond differently, the stronger the bonds between the new neurons grow, the less effort is required as the old connections wither and die until it actually becomes easy. And voilà, a new habit is formed.

HEY, THIS DOESN'T FEEL GOOD!

*We don't stop because [we're] incapable of
continuing, but because the effort required to
continue is greater than we're willing to exert.*
—ALEX HUTCHINSON

Yes, your first attempts to respond differently than you normally would will feel uncomfortable, weird, awkward, and definitely not satisfying. But don't ignore or fight the discomfort. Instead, acknowledge and feel your frustration. Unless you give voice to your feelings, you're apt to fall prey to anything that offers temporary relief, like a shopping spree, an eating binge, or various other addictions.

Nir Eyal, in his book *Indistractable*, describes a smoking cessation study in which, as quoted in the *Wall Street Journal*, "participants who acknowledged and explored their cravings quit at double the rate of those in the American Lung Association's best-performing program."[2] Honoring your feelings, as I've mentioned throughout this book, is fundamental to both financial and personal health.

I recently got an email from an attorney and former client, Cindy Lou, who came to me frustrated with her inability to reach her personal or financial potential.

"Your *biggest* gift to me was your admonition to commit myself to being uncomfortable for the sake of financial growth and, to a certain extent, self-respect. In my case, that willingness to be uncomfortable took the form of asking for more money even when there was a clear possibility—even likelihood—of disappointment.

"I set a goal of $100,000 in billings for this year. I raised my prices. I didn't back down when someone got upset or angry or said they couldn't afford me. It was really hard, but I made myself. And I am happy to tell you I had exceeded that goal by the end of May."

I was thrilled to hear about her success. However, the real payoff for constant repetition, despite the discomfort, was revealed in her final sentences.

"*What's more, being uncomfortable is no longer very uncomfortable.* Disappointments and even outright refusals or rejections now feel like part of the landscape instead of the monumental cliffs I had imagined them to be before."

What once took intense effort became a nonissue for Cindy Lou. Just as it will for you.

FOUR PRACTICES FOR CONTINUALLY RESPONDING DIFFERENTLY

To help strengthen your resolve and not succumb to the old wiring, here are four practices you can use to support your initial efforts to repeatedly respond differently.

1. **Watch Your Words**
2. **Visualize**
3. **Meditate**
4. **Celebrate**

Practice 1: Watch Your Words

*We don't describe the world we see, but see the world
we describe. We see only what we talk about.*
—JOSEPH JAWORSKI

Phil Hellmuth is a professional poker player who has, as of
this writing, won a record 14 World Series of Poker. But prior
to that he suffered an eight-year losing streak. No matter what
he did, his bad luck wasn't budging. Then one day he changed
a few words he regularly used and his life turned around. He
altered his email address from "tryingtobethegreatest" to
"beingthegreatest." To date he's won over $22 million.

"I wasn't winning anything," he told a *Wall Street Journal*
reporter. "Then I just started smashing it. I'm a big believer in
the power of your own words."[3]

Language has a profound impact on your brain. Whatever you repeat often enough, even if it's a lie, will eventually
become your truth. Negative words mobilize the fear center of the brain, increasing stress and anxiety. Positive words
activate the rational brain, producing a general sense of
well-being.

As Andrew Newberg and Mark Robert Waldman wrote
in their book *Words Can Change Your Brain*, "By holding a
positive and optimistic word in your mind, you stimulate
frontal lobe activity. This area includes specific language centers that connect directly to the motor cortex responsible for
moving you into action."[4]

I discovered the weight my words carried years ago, when
I was going through a very rough patch in my life. My therapist gave me an assignment.

"For two weeks," she told me, "I want you to observe your conversations, without changing a thing."

I was aghast when I realized how often I put myself down, without even realizing it. I'd dismiss my skills ("Oh, that's no big thing"), deflect praise ("I thought I was awful"), and diminish my successes ("But I could've done so much better").

"Self-depreciation is your comfort zone," she told me. What felt like humility was, in truth, wreaking havoc on my self-esteem, eroding my self-confidence.

"What you share you strengthen," explains *A Course in Miracles.*[5] No wonder I was struggling. I immediately instructed some friends, "When you hear me putting myself down, call me on it." And they did. I was struck by how different I felt just by changing the language I used.

I again witnessed the power of words during the depth of the dot-com bust in 2001. I noticed I was having very different conversations with high earners than with their lower-paid peers. Underearners were constantly grumbling about the lousy economy and the lack of jobs. They refused to believe life could possibly improve, so why even try. But the high earners, even those who had been hit by hard times, were surprisingly upbeat about the opportunities that were out there and their likelihood of finding success.

I saw how each person's reality directly reflected their differing perspectives. Their words became self-fulfilling prophecies. George Orwell once said, "If you want to control people's thoughts, commandeer their words." So too, if you want to control your thoughts and feelings (which, as we've seen, are directly responsible for sculpting your brain), be hypervigilant about the words you use.

From this moment on, talk only about what you're committed to, not what you're worried about. Stop apologizing unnecessarily or belittling yourself in any way. Speak about the life you desire to create, who you want to be, how you'd love to feel. And for heaven's sake, Stop. Telling. Your. Old. Story. This is always my first order of business with clients.

"If you keep talking about your past," I say emphatically, "I guarantee you'll continue to repeat it. On the other hand, every time you talk about your dreams and aspirations, you literally weaken the old dysfunctional neuropathways and strengthen new, more desirable ones."

I was on the phone with Joyce Griggs after she'd just given away most of her belongings in preparation to move to Greece. When I asked how she felt, her response was striking. "Uncertainty is my friend. I'm excited to see what happens in my life as I make this transition."

Even after her travel plans were suspended indefinitely by the coronavirus, she remained calm, embracing uncertainty, emailing her Greek friends and eagerly anticipating the lifting of restrictions, which she kept reminding herself would happen eventually.

Remember Patti Fagan, whose mother rejected and shamed her because she was the product of an unwanted pregnancy? She worked hard on rewiring those feelings by repeating an affirmation: "God chose me."

Be warned, however. Those old neuropathways you thought had withered away could suddenly reappear. Repeating affirmations—short statements declaring what you want as if it's already yours—are like waving a magic wand. Eventually the unwanted behaviors will disappear. And you don't even have to believe the affirmations are true. The power is in the repetition.

During our interview, I asked Patti if feelings of rejection ever come up anymore.

"Oh yeah, but not very often," she laughed. "A couple of weeks ago, I went with my husband to a dinner where all the dentists bring their spouses. I caught myself thinking *I'm going to be rejected. I don't know anyone and I'm not going to have anyone to talk to.*"

She immediately recognized she was repeating her old story. "I thought, 'Wait a minute! If they reject me, who cares?' I was needing everyone to accept me. But I realized that not everyone's going to accept me and that's okay. God has chosen me." She ended up having a marvelous time.

(Note: Affirmations only work if what you *say* you want is what you *really* want. If you're not having success with them, I suggest you reread Chapter 8 and do the resistance work.)

Rewire in Action

WHAT AM I SAYING?

Spend a week observing your conversations. Start noticing what you talk about and how you're feeling. Don't change anything, don't try to edit what comes out of your mouth. Then ask yourself this question: Is what I'm sharing with others how I want to wire my brain?

The following week, consciously choose to only talk about possibilities, not problems; about what you aspire to achieve, rather than everything that is going (or could go) wrong. Talk as if you're a powerful adult, not a hapless victim. How does this feel? What do you notice?

(continued)

Is your speaking reflecting the decisions you've made or the fear that you feel?

When you do this, you'll likely feel strange, awkward, somewhat arrogant, and probably phony (especially if you're hanging out with negative folks). But, that's exactly how rewiring feels—like "this isn't me."

Do the same thing with the conversation going on in your head, the little voices telling you what you can and can't do, urging you to play small, be safe, hold back. We are by far the worst naysayers we'll ever encounter. Thank those voices for sharing, and start a new conversation based on what you've learned from this book.

Practice 2: Visualize

You don't have to move an inch to drive
positive plastic changes in your brain.
—MICHAEL MERZENICH

In 1994, a Harvard neuroscientist made a stunning discovery—visualization, or mental rehearsal, changed the physical structure of the brain, without anyone actually having to do anything.[6]

Dr. Alvaro Pascual-Leone had a group of volunteers practice a simple song on the piano for two hours a day over a five-day period. He told another group to practice the same song for the same amount of time. But with one big difference: he instructed the second group to hold their hands still and simply imagine how they would move their fingers. Brain image data revealed that the area of the brain that controlled the finger movements was enlarged in both groups, whether they were imagining or actually playing the piano.

This is exciting news.

Repetition, whether real or imagined, is equally effective at creating new neural circuits. By merely visualizing yourself doing something—like giving a captivating presentation or setting up an automatic savings plan—you actually strengthen the same neuropathways without having to physically perform.

"The brain is changed by internal mental rehearsal in the same ways and involving precisely the same processes that control changes achieved through interaction with the external world," explains acclaimed neuroscientist Dr. Michael Merzenich.[7]

Rebecca, an executive vice president of an accounting firm, wanted my help in asking for a raise. She came across as a strong, confident woman. She also firmly believed she deserved that raise since she'd been there for years without any increase in salary, but she was seriously intimidated by her difficult boss.

"He's such an imposing man. And he's so abrupt," she said in an uncharacteristically halting manner. "I literally lose my voice when I'm around him."

I assigned her the standard homework: research the going rate for positions like hers, document her contributions to the company, compose a script, and practice with a friend. We also explored how her past might be affecting her reaction to her boss. Months later, she still wasn't able to work up the courage to make the request.

Finally, I got an idea, and she was game. I asked her to close her eyes and picture herself walking into her boss's office, dressed to the nines, feeling poised, powerful, full of confidence, and actually excited to ask for a raise because she knew she was worth it. She continued doing this visualization daily, putting as much positive emotion into it as she possibly could.

In our next appointment, I could hear the excitement in her voice. "I wasn't nervous at all," she declared. "I'm so proud of myself. I asked for what I wanted and told him why I deserved it. It felt really good. And I could tell he was impressed." She paused, but was still upbeat when she told me he had refused her request because of budgetary restraints. Instead of crumbling in defeat, she stayed surprisingly motivated.

"I said to him, 'I understand. What can I do to get a raise in the future?'" They brainstormed what he needed to do, things she could do, and agreed to revisit the issue in three months. She was thrilled. Sure, she didn't get what she wanted right away, but repeatedly visualizing the conversation significantly boosted her confidence, allowed her to bond with her boss, and kept the door open for future discussions. Less than a year later, she got her raise.

• Rewire in Action •

PERFECT DAY VISUALIZATION

I want you to get comfortable and begin to picture your perfect day. See yourself waking up in the morning, excited to start your day. Take in your surroundings. Are you with someone or alone? Once you get moving, where do you go? What do you do? Who do you interact with? What activities do you engage in that give you great joy and satisfaction? Imagine this day in vivid detail and feel the pleasure it gives you. As the day comes to a close, where do you go? With whom? What do you do about dinner? Do you do anything afterward? Then it's time to get ready for bed. As you fall asleep, review your day and the happiness it brought you.

Practice 3: Meditate

> *Meditation is not a way of making your mind quiet. It's a way of entering into the quiet that's already there—buried under the 50,000 thoughts the average person thinks every day.*
> —DEEPAK CHOPRA

Extensive research has proven that, aside from toxins and injuries, nothing damages your brain more than stress.

"Chronic stress can lead to a rut in the brain in which the wiring of our neural networks keeps us repeating the same dysfunctional behavior," writes neurologist David Perlmutter in *Power Up Your Brain*. "Because of the way our brains have been wired by stress or trauma, we're unable to think or feel our way out of a crisis. So, we keep recreating early experiences over and over."[8]

When under stress, your brain will always default to the strongest pathways and actually kill off the weaker ones, preventing you from responding differently.

Practicing mindful meditation on a regular basis, however, has been proven to significantly lower stress. In a 2015 Harvard Study, neuroscientist Sarah Lazar found that meditating for 5 to 10 minutes a day changes the neocortex, improving memory, resilience to stress, decision making, and well-being.[9]

"It's a form of mental exercise, really," Dr. Lazar told a reporter for the *Washington Post*. "And just as exercise increases health, helps us handle stress better and promotes longevity, meditation confers some of those same benefits."

Mindful meditation is, indeed, an exercise in calming your mind and relaxing your body. But beyond that, meditation is unsurpassable for training your mind to focus, which is a prerequisite to rewiring.

In short, mindful meditation means observing and accepting thoughts and feelings without judgment. There are many ways to do this. The one I find easiest yet very effective is to sit quietly and focus on your breath, a mantra, an image in your head, or an actual object, like a candle. When thoughts pop up, as they always do, redirect your attention back to your breath or whatever you're concentrating on, without any mental commentary. I love science writer Sharon Begley's suggestion to react "to intruding thoughts [as if] they're a butterfly floating into your field of vision."[10]

People often think meditating means eliminating all thoughts, but that's a myth insists Daniel Goleman in his excellent book *Altered Traits: Science Reveals How Meditation Changes Your Mind, Brain, and Body*.[11] "Your mind must wander in order for meditation to have the training effect. Every time you bring your mind back to your meditation, you make the neural circuitry in your brain a little stronger."

As Dr. Goleman points out: "The same circuitry in the brain that focuses attention also manages the amygdala, which causes you to get anxious, upset or depressed. [Meditators] have a double benefit: They react less strongly to things that used to upset them and recover more quickly when they do get upset."

Rewire in Action

MEDITATION PRACTICE

Set a timer for 5 minutes. Sit in a comfortable position while concentrating on your in-breath and out-breath. You can repeat the mantra: "I'm breathing in. I'm breathing out" with each inhale and exhale. Or try counting each breath. When your mind wanders, bring it back to your breath or start counting from the beginning.

Practice 4: Celebrate

You are allowed to be both a masterpiece and
a work in progress, simultaneously.
—SOPHIA BUSH

Here's a question for you. When was the last time you celebrated or even acknowledged yourself for responding differently or making even the tiniest bit of progress, despite the difficulty? Sadly, the answer for most will be "rarely."

Positive reinforcement—anything from patting yourself on the back to popping open the bubbly—works for one simple fact. Rewarding yourself feels good. And any pleasant sensation triggers the release of pleasurable chemicals, like dopamine, encouraging the brain to keep repeating the behavior.

"It's no secret that we derive pleasure from doing things we enjoy," said neuroscientist Rui Costa, CEO of Columbia's Zuckerman Institute. "The brain learns which activity patterns lead to feel-good sensations and reshapes itself to more efficiently reproduce those patterns."[12] It's why teachers give kids gold stars and cute stickers to encourage behaviors that may not come naturally or feel good right away.

Rewiring for wealth is anything but pleasurable in the beginning because it often requires delayed gratification. There's no immediate reward for spending less, saving more, or investing wisely. But the intrinsic payoff for dining out, buying a new pair of shoes, or traveling to Tahiti is instantaneous.

However, with repetition, wealth-building activities will eventually become gratifying in themselves. But until they do, they need to be positively reinforced.

As Stanford University psychologist Kelly McGonigal wrote in *The Willpower Instinct*, "Celebrating tells your brain a behavior is beneficial, and that it should look for more opportunities to engage in it."[13]

Dr. Merzenich, known as the father of neuroplasticity, is a big proponent of celebrating and appreciating yourself. "Count every little indication of progress as success and reward yourself, in your mind, for those growing achievements," he says, explaining that the more positive you feel about an activity, "the more your brain has been turning on its *Save-it* machinery."[14]

These four practices (Watch Your Words, Visualize, Meditate, and Celebrate), when used consistently, in conjunction with the other two Power Tools (Resistance Work and Reparenting), are like little machetes, quickly clearing any deep-rooted, unwanted neuropathways, prompting new ones to sprout in their place.

CARMELA'S STORY

You are very powerful, provided you
know how powerful you are.
—YOGI BHAJAN

Carmela grew up impoverished, lived in the projects, married a successful lawyer, and 34 years later, received a multimillion-dollar divorce settlement. But by the time she joined Rewire, most of the money was gone. Though she was a sophisticated, accomplished professional, she never looked at her financial statements, had no idea what she spent, and was $8,000 in debt. I assumed the cause of her troubles would be found in her upbringing.

"My parents thought money was an ugly burden," she recalled, in a thick New York accent. "They were always angry. I grew up in fear. They never said 'you can do anything' or told me I was great or smart or anything positive. They said they didn't want me to get a swelled head. They thought the world was a dangerous place, where I could get hurt. I realize I'm saying stuff like that to myself all the time."

Clearly, Carmela's brain had been hardwired to see only fear and scarcity. Even when she had millions in the bank and a house in the Hamptons, she said, "I was still financially insecure." She stubbornly kept telling her old story: *"I'm not enough." "I'll never have enough." "I'm not worth it." "I don't deserve it."*

When I led her through a reparenting visualization, something shifted. "I never heard how scared little Carmela was," Carmela said. "I'm realizing my fear of showing up in the world is my child's, not mine. I'm telling her what I never heard: 'You can do anything.' I told her she's safe, that I'll take care of her from now on."

"You know what that means, Carmela," I said. "From here on out, you must consistently respond differently. Repetition is the key to permanently wiring in those new beliefs. Let me suggest four practices that will help."

Introducing Practice 1, Watch Your Words, I told her: "I want you to pay attention to your words. Every time you open your mouth, you have a choice: repeat your story of 'not enough' or talk about how excited you are to become financially savvy and successful."

Her energy was completely different when we next spoke. "I feel like I'm shaking off cobwebs by watching what I say. I'm starting to use a whole new vocabulary, especially in the way I talk to myself."

Excited to try Practice 2, Visualize, she visualized herself "taking the stage of a very large workshop, putting together a large coalition of women to promote it. I have a lot to say. And people respond."

Practice 3, Meditate, seemed to come naturally. She reduced her pace significantly, taking time to meditate, do yoga. "I got quiet and stopped all the running around. Slowing down gave me a chance to focus on what I wanted to do."

Then she began Practice 4, Celebrate. "I'm taking time to appreciate who I am and what I've done, telling myself things like "Good job.' 'You've come a long way,' " she said proudly.

"People have said positive things to me, but I couldn't hear it. Now I can. Even better, I am experiencing my own value. I've gotten awards. I've been the associate producer on two major movies. I accomplished this without any encouragement."

One day, she reported, these words came to her: *I'm the one I've been waiting for.* "That's my new mantra," she enthused. "To be fully myself and love myself. I trust everything is in place and I'm safe to move forward."

During this period, she fell in love with a very smart and supportive man who's helping her start her own seminar business. "He really believes in me. I'm no longer dimming my light. I'm free to be who I am. Everyone is saying Alan is so lucky to have me. And I tell myself, 'Take it in, Carmela. Let yourself hear it.'"

With a new sense of self-esteem, she felt like a different person. "The feeling of being unworthy caused me to avoid money," she realized. "But the only way to stay on top of it is to look at it."

Carmela eagerly began tracking her spending ("It was confronting, but I'll have my debt paid off by December."), did a budget ("First time ever.") and met with an advisor ("We redid my accounts to make sure they're diversified.")

Her life only got better. "I'm not wallowing in my past at all. I realized I can put that to rest," she said, neatly summarizing the rewiring process—putting unwanted parts of your past to rest and waking up to a brighter future.

11

DIRECTING YOUR DESTINY

Destiny is not a matter of chance; it is a matter of choice.
It is not a thing to be waited for, it is a thing to be achieved.
—WILLIAM JENNINGS BRYAN

AND SO IT EVOLVES . . .

Your thoughts are the architects of your destiny.
—DAVID O. MCKAY

As we come to the end of our time together, allow me to share a line from Joseph Jaworski's incredible book *Source*: "The next phase of human evolution is that of fully conscious beings who are directing their own destinies and the destinies of the world around them."[1]

Those words, dear reader, convey the ultimate purpose of this book. Wealth building, in the context of rewiring, is but a metaphor for personal transformation, a Heroine's Journey to find your Soul's path. By combining neuroscience, psychology, spirituality, and personal finance, I've given you a self-directed process to train your mind to reprogram your brain and empower you to consciously direct your destiny.

While this book has laid out a step-by-step plan with the main goal of improving your finances by amassing more than enough, it does much more than that. The financial independence you create gives you a distinct advantage when pursuing your dreams. It also wakens you to your authentic nature and the person you were born to be before the world began indoctrinating you with its lies, half-truths, and other misinformation.

Admittedly, rewiring is not easy. Nor is it comfortable. But it is well worth the effort. To become your true Self means shining your light brightly, spreading your wings boldly, and soaring far beyond your limiting beliefs to do what you're here on this earth to do. What could possibly be a greater accomplishment or grander privilege than that?

The world desperately needs awakened beings—both women and men—to help heal the misery and pain, divisiveness and discord, inequality and intolerance that is afflicting this planet. But first each of us must heal those afflictions within ourselves, which is the work we've been doing throughout this book. I leave you with one last story—before getting to your own—of a woman convinced she was powerless until she learned how to direct her destiny by following the three steps of The Rewire Response.

DIONNE'S STORY

*First become a blessing to yourself so that
you may become a blessing to others.*
—RABBI SAMSON RAPHAEL HIRSCH

One day after an exceptionally fun Zumba class, I rushed up to thank the instructor. She looked at me oddly, then burst into tears. I don't remember ever eliciting such a response from anyone.

"I was just watching your videos on YouTube," she sobbed. "I need your help."

And that was how I met Dionne Thomas, a fitness instructor who loved her work but had a body that felt battered, a calendar that was crammed full, and a bank account that was near empty.

"I'm living hand-to-mouth," she told me, trying to pull herself together. "I'm at my wits end. I can't keep going on like this."

Two weeks later, I was on the phone with Dionne for our first session. I'd just begun bringing neuroscience into my work, making her, one could say, an unwitting but eager guinea pig.

"I teach at gyms and rent space in studios. I'm always running around trying to get people to sign up. I get so caught up serving others and making sure everyone's happy that I put myself on the back burner and work myself to the ground," she told me. "I avoid thinking about money because it seems so overwhelming. I have nothing in savings. Nothing."

"Let's talk about what you *do* want," I said, posing the Power Question, which I posed to you earlier when I had you write down your intention for reading this book. I told her this question—*What do I want?*—is the first step toward consciously training your mind to direct your destiny.

"This is tough," Dionne griped, but after a few minutes, she spoke up. "I want to serve more people all over the country. I don't care about helping them lose weight. I want to help them connect to their souls, their authenticity, and their joy, through movement." She then added emphatically, "I definitely want to lead a balanced life."

She took a deep breath and continued, "I want to come out of vagueness about money." And she wanted to "clean up the mess" of not paying taxes in 2010. "I know I need to talk to someone," she explained. "But I'm so ashamed. All I do is beat myself up."

Dionne grew up poor, watching her beloved mother come home late at night, worn out from working long hours to support her children. "She lived a hard life. She was always in pain. I remember just wanting to make everything okay, but I couldn't." The trauma of watching her mother suffer left Dionne with a deep sense of powerlessness.

Her early wiring became obvious with her next words. "There was never enough. No matter what you do, you have to keep working until you're exhausted."

"That's the same story you're replaying to this day," I noted gently. "So that's what we are going to rewire." Thus began our passage through The Rewire Response. I relished watching Dionne dig deep to ferret out the truth. When I interviewed her a few years later, I was speaking to a very different woman.

"Working with you, I realized I was so focused on everyone else, but what was I doing for me except beating myself up? Just seeing my behavior in an objective way was the start of me making changes," she said.

It didn't take long for Dionne to recognize how bru-
tally she was abusing herself through an incessant stream of
vicious self-talk.

"I never realized that my drug of choice was beating
myself up. I was trying to avoid pain by causing pain, like
a cutter," she acknowledged. After Step 1, recognizing her
unhealthy thoughts, she then reflected on the next two steps,
reframing and responding differently: "I've learned to resist
the urge to beat myself up by consciously being gentle with
myself. I take my young Dionne for walks on the beach, telling her everything is going to be okay. This always puts me
in a better place. I've been able to confidently move forward
instead of constantly bemoaning where I *should* be."

During our work together, Dionne also began a relationship that quickly grew serious, but he lived in another city
and wanted her to move. She was torn because she longed
to live closer to him, but she also hated the thought of leaving her many friends and devoted students. "I loved my life. I
didn't want to leave." Underneath, of course, lay the burning
question: What if it doesn't work out?

As she struggled to come to a decision, she asked herself a different question: "One of my biggest takeaways from
you was to ask myself the most important question for me,
which is 'What do I really want?' My first reaction was always
I can't have that. It's not for me. I'm not one of them," she
recalled, until she understood these were erroneous messages
imprinted in childhood. "When I take time to really sit with
that question now, I get to the heart of the matter instead of
just being on the autopilot of deprivation."

She was able to follow her heart and make the move when
she reframed her fear. "I'm not leaving. I'm moving toward

something better," she told herself. "It's a choice I'm making. I'm willing to take a chance. If it doesn't work out, I'll be sad. I'll grieve the loss. But I'll be fine. I can rebuild my life wherever I want. I'd *never* had those thoughts before."

It took time for her to find her footing in a strange city. But when I interviewed her, she was working far fewer hours—"I have the lightest schedule ever. My body feels good."—making a lot more money, teaching Zumba classes in corporations and high-end gyms and offering workshops, just as she'd long dreamed, combining joyful dance moves, soul connecting exercises, and personal healing.

I can't help but attribute her success to another profound recognition. "I realized that I'd been holding onto lack to stay connected to my family. It made me so sad, feeling like I am different than them," she said, describing the bittersweet process of individuation. "I don't feel that way anymore. I see the difference in their thinking and living and how far I've come. I have better things to do with my money than rob Peter to pay Paul. I don't want to pass this family legacy of lack on to my kids."

"Remember how you kept yourself in scarcity by never filling your gas tank to full?" I reminded her, laughing.

"Yeah, I'd only get enough gas to get me through a few days, just enough to get by. But I had a massive shift in thinking," she said, also laughing. "Just the other day my mom picked me up at the airport with my car. I stopped for gas even though there was half a tank left. She was shocked. Having a full tank was a foreign concept to Mom. It's what rich people do. I told her that's my way to stay in abundance. My old way was always running on empty. Now I know I'm not going to empty my savings, just like I won't empty my gas tank. That's my new normal." She happily, gratefully shared everything she'd learned about rewiring with her mother and her children, a both generous and genius gesture. What you share with another, you strengthen in yourself.

Dionne was rightfully proud of the progress she'd made since we first met. "I feel like I'm setting myself up for success, doing my heart's work, eating well, and feeling secure. I'm no longer stressed out about money because I'm taking care of it. I've *never* loved or trusted myself so much," she said, excited to tell me she'd broken her old pattern of avoidance by consistently responding differently than she used to.

"I've learned that taking care of things as they come up instead of having a big dark cloud hanging over me is so freeing, so life changing," she exclaimed. "I got my taxes taken care of. I had so much resistance. But I went through it. And I hardly owed any money. The lesson for me was that so much of what I've been scared of and didn't want to face has been nothing. The frenzy was worse than the facing."

She had just returned from a Zumba conference in Orlando where, she told me, "I spent less than $100, even though there were all these fancy new clothes I wanted. But I'm so conscious of spending now. And it doesn't feel like deprivation. It's like the concept of the gas tank. It feels so much better having money in the bank than barely getting by. I never want to deplete myself again, in any way."

There are still times, she admitted, when she slips into "a momentary fear of lack. But when that happens, I remind myself that I create my reality. I created lack when I told myself I couldn't have something, or I'd avoid something because it was scary or hard. If I created lack, I can also create abundance."

I knew she fully grasped the true meaning of wealth when she told me, "I used to think abundance was a certain amount of money that I could never achieve. But having more than enough feels really abundant. And I feel like the more I allow money in and pay attention to it, the more I'll have."

She concluded our conversation saying, "I'm in a great place. I'll have slipups. I don't expect myself to be perfect. But I won't get caught up in my own crap like I had for years. It's not who I am anymore."

Like Dionne, everyone begins the rewiring process in some degree of distress or despair. And like Dionne, those who commit to stay the course and exert the effort wind up sounding like a Greek chorus singing the same tune: "That's not who I am anymore."

ONCE UPON A TIME

I am larger, better than I thought. I did
not know I held so much goodness.
—WALT WHITMAN

I like to think of *Rewire for Wealth* as a work of nonfiction paving the way for your fairy-tale ending that, through the miracle of mind training, can actually, inevitably come true. An ending that would go something like this:

> *. . . and she lived happily ever after. Not because she found her Prince. But because she discovered her Power. A Power that had lain dormant within, her entire life, until the day fate intervened. That was the day she stumbled upon a formula for rewiring her brain. It was as if she (not her fairy godmother) cast*

a magic spell and she fell deeply in love with someone she knew she could count on forever . . . herself. From that day forward, money ceased to be a source of stress or distraction but became a tool for enriching her life as well as making a difference in the lives of others.

I conclude with a final exercise. I want you to write your new story.

● Rewire in Action ●

WRITE YOUR NEW STORY

In this final exercise, you will write your new story by completing the sentence below: "And I am living happily ever after because . . ."

I want you to briefly describe the life you crave, not the one you're living. It may involve a total makeover or small modifications in a few different areas.

Notice if your thoughts tell you it's not practical or even plausible. Know that's your brain defaulting to old neuropathways. Resist the urge to acquiesce.

Consider the legacy you wish to leave. Allow your imagination to run wild, to dream audaciously. Make it fun, as if you're a child playing make-believe.

Ignore your Ego's shrieks, *"You can't do that. Who do you think you are?"* Keep reminding yourself, "I'm making a conscious choice to direct my own destiny."

"And I am living happily ever after because _____

_____

_____

Let this story become your new reality. Trust it is your intended future yearning to emerge. Allow the words to sink into your psyche. Adopt them as your new mantra. Repeat this story often (especially when you are tempted to tell your old one). Focus on it in meditation. Visualize it as you fall asleep.

Recognize any negative reactions and quickly reframe them. When making pertinent decisions, respond differently than you normally would, despite the discomfort. Above all, presume it will come to pass. Positive expectation, according to research, is more powerful than a strong desire for rewiring your brain.

Rest assured. This new story is not some grandiose tale told by your insecure Ego, but guidance from your loving Soul, urging you to step into your Greatness and inspire others to do the same. This is what it means to become a shining light in a world seeped in darkness. This is what will happen when you *Rewire for Wealth*.

NOTES

CHAPTER 1

1. Fidelity Investments, *Fidelity Investments Money FIT Women Study: Executive Summary*, 2015, https://www.fidelity.com/bin-public/060 _www_fidelity_com/documents/women-fit-money-study.pdf.

2. Jeffrey Schwartz and Rebecca Gladding, *You Are Not Your Brain: The 4-Step Solution for Changing Bad Habits, Ending Unhealthy Thinking, and Taking Control of Your Life* (Avery, 2012).

3. 2018 JPMorgan Chase study reported in Colleen Briggs and Heather McCulloch, "Closing the Women's Wealth Gap," JPMorgan Chase & Co Women on the Move, March 28, 2018, https:// www.jpmorganchase.com/corporate/news/insights/cbriggs-closing -the-womens-wealth-gap.htm.

4. Lorna Sabbia and Maddy Dychtwald, *Women & Financial Wellness: Beyond the Bottom Line*, a Merrill Lynch study conducted in partnership with AGE WAVE, https://www.bofaml.com/content/dam /boamlimages/documents/articles/ID18_0244/ml_womens_study .pdf.

5. Thomas J. Stanley, *The Millionaire Next Door: The Surprising Secrets of America's Rich*, twentieth anniversary edition (Taylor Trade Publishing, 2016).

6. Fidelity Investments, *Fidelity Investments Money FIT Women Study: Executive Summary*, 2015, https://www.fidelity.com/bin-public/060 _www_fidelity_com/documents/women-fit-money-study.pdf.

7. Norman Doidge, *The Brain That Changes Itself: Stories of Personal Triumph from the Frontiers of Brain Science*, reprint edition (Penguin Books, 2007).
8. Richard O'Connor, *Rewire: Change Your Brain to Break Bad Habits, Overcome Addictions, Conquer Self-Destructive Behavior* (Plume, 2015).
9. Andrew Newberg, *How God Changes Your Brain: Breakthrough Findings from a Leading Neuroscientist* (Ballantine Books, 2010).
10. Joe Dispenza, *You Are the Placebo: Making Your Mind Matter* (Hay House Inc, 2015).

CHAPTER 2

1. Jeffrey Schwartz, *The Mind and the Brain: Neuroplasticity and the Power of Mental Force* (Harper Perennial, 2003).
2. John Arden, *Rewire Your Brain: Think Your Way to a Better Life* (Wiley, 2010).
3. Rick Hanson, *Buddha's Brain: The Practical Neuroscience of Happiness, Love, and Wisdom* (New Harbinger Publications, 2009).
4. Sharon Begley, *Train Your Mind, Change Your Brain: How a New Science Reveals Our Extraordinary Potential to Transform Ourselves* (Ballantine Books, 2007).
5. Lachlan Gilbert, "Don't Even Think About It: Why Thought Control Is So Difficult," Medical Xpress, April 30, 2019, https://medicalxpress.com/news/2019-04-dont-thought-difficult.html.
6. Jeffrey Schwartz, *The Mind and the Brain: Neuroplasticity and the Power of Mental Force* (Harper Perennial, 2003).
7. Foundation for Inner Peace, *A Course in Miracles: Combined Volume* (The Foundation for Inner Peace, 1975).
8. Dr. Bessel van der Kolk, *The Body Keeps the Score: Brain, Mind, and Body in the Healing of Trauma* (Penguin Books, 2015).
9. The Center for Healing Shame, founded by Sheila Rubin and Bret Lyon, is an international education center supporting therapists and other helping professionals to understand and transform client shame (see https://healingshame.com/).
10. Matt Swayne, "Suppressing Negative Emotions During Health Scare May Whip up Spiral of Fear," Penn State News, July 10, 2018, https://news.psu.edu/story/527591/2018/07/10/research/suppressing -negative-emotions-during-health-scare-may-whip-spiral.

11. Van der Kolk, *The Body Keeps the Score.*
12. Adele Atkinson and Flore-Anne Messy, A study of financial literacy in 12 countries, sponsored by International Network on Financial Education, *Journal of Pension Economics and Finance,* October 2011.
13. A 2013 study of 1,542 Australian women, by Farrell, Fry, and Risse, reported in *Journal of Economic Psychology,* July 2015, https://www.researchgate.net/publication/271707546_The_significance_of_financial_self-efficacy_in_explaining_women's_personal_finance_behaviour.

CHAPTER 3

1. Charles Duhigg, *The Power of Habit: Why We Do What We Do in Life and Business* (Random House, 2012).
2. Patience Haggin, "Can't Save Money? You Can Blame Your Brain," *Wall Street Journal,* November 28, 2018.
3. Benjamin Graham, *The Intelligent Investor: The Definitive Book on Value Investing* (Harper Business, revised, subsequent edition, 2006).
4. Benjamin Snyder, "7 Insights from Legendary Investor Warren Buffet," CNBC, May 1, 2017, https://www.cnbc.com/2017/05/01/7-insights-from-legendary-investor-warren-buffett.html.
5. Graham, *The Intelligent Investor.*
6. James Mackintosh, "The False Prophet of 'Long-Term Investing,'" *Wall Street Journal,* October 9, 2017.
7. Burton G. Malkiel, "How to Invest in an Overpriced World," WSJ Opinion, January 22, 2018, https://www.wsj.com/articles/how-to-invest-in-an-overpriced-world-1516666457.

CHAPTER 4

1. Jeffrey Schwartz, *The Mind and the Brain: Neuroplasticity and the Power of Mental Force* (Harper Perennial, 2003).
2. Victor Rivero, "What Is Unlearning: Roundtable Interview," EDTECH Digest, July 13, 2017, https://edtechdigest.com/2017/07/13/what-is-unlearning/.
3. Foundation for Inner Peace, *A Course in Miracles: Combined Volume* (The Foundation for Inner Peace, 1975).
4. Schwartz, *The Mind and the Brain.*

5. Bessel van der Kolk, *The Body Keeps the Score: Brain, Mind, and Body in the Healing of Trauma* (Penguin Books, 2015).
6. John B. Arden, *Rewire Your Brain: Think Your Way to a Better Life* (Wiley, 2010).

CHAPTER 5

1. Neuroskeptic, "The 70,000 Thoughts per Day Myth?," *Discover* magazine, May 9, 2012, https://www.discovermagazine.com/mind/the-70-000-thoughts-per-day-myth.
2. Jeffrey Schwartz, *The Mind and the Brain: Neuroplasticity and the Power of Mental Force* (Harper Perennial, 2003).
3. Richard O'Connor Ph.D., *Rewire: Change Your Brain to Break Bad Habits, Overcome Addictions, Conquer Self-Destructive Behavior* (Plume, 2015).
4. Schwartz, *The Mind and the Brain.*
5. David Eagleman, *The Brain: The Story of You* (Vintage, 2015).
6. Elizabeth Bernstein, "Find Compassion for Difficult People," *Wall Street Journal*, July 31, 2017.
7. Schwartz, *The Mind and the Brain.*
8. "Words of Wisdom: No Self, No Problem," *The Wise Brain Bulletin* 2, no. 11 (November 2008), https://www.wisebrain.org/WBB2_11.pdf.

CHAPTER 6

1. Joseph Jaworski, *Synchronicity: The Inner Path of Leadership* (BK, 1994).
2. Jeffrey Schwartz, *The Mind and the Brain: Neuroplasticity and the Power of Mental Force* (Harper Perennial, 2003).
3. Jeffrey M. Schwartz and Rebecca Gladding, *You Are Not Your Brain: The 4-Step Solution for Changing Bad Habits, Ending Unhealthy Thinking, and Taking Control of Your Life* (Avery, 2012).
4. Rick Hanson, *Buddha's Brain: The Practical Neuroscience of Happiness, Love, and Wisdom* (New Harbinger Publications, 2009).
5. Jeffrey M. Schwartz, *Brain Lock: Free Yourself from Obsessive-Compulsive Behavior: A Four-Step Self-Treatment Method to Change Your Brain Chemistry*, twentieth anniversary edition (HarperCollins, 2016).
6. Debbie Ford, *The Dark Side of the Light Chasers* (Hay House, 2011).

7. Michael Merzenich, *Soft-Wired: How the New Science of Brain Plasticity Can Change Your Life* (Parnassus Publishing, 2013).

8. Eleanor Brownn, "The OTHER Serenity Prayer," http://www.eleanorbrownn.com/.

CHAPTER 7

1. Jeffrey M. Schwartz and Rebecca Gladding, *You Are Not Your Brain: The 4-Step Solution for Changing Bad Habits, Ending Unhealthy Thinking, and Taking Control of Your Life* (Avery, 2012).

2. "Learning to Deal with the Imposter Syndrome," *New York Times*, October 26, 2015.

3. Joseph Jaworski, *Synchronicity: The Inner Path of Leadership* (Berrett-Koehler Publishers, 1996).

4. "8 Ways to Be Kinder to Yourself in 2020," *New York Times*, December 24, 2019, https://www.nytimes.com/2019/12/24/smarter-living/8-ways-to-be-kinder-to-yourself-in-2020.html.

5. Joe Dispenza, *Breaking the Habit of Being Yourself* (Hay House Inc., 2012).

Chapter 8

1. Lauren Suval, "The Question of Forgiveness," Psych Central.com, July 8, 2018, https://psychcentral.com/blog/the-question-of-forgiveness/.

CHAPTER 9

1. Stephen A. Diamond, "Essential Secrets of Psychotherapy: The Inner Child," Psychology Today, June 7, 2008, https://www.psychologytoday.com/us/blog/evil-deeds/200806/essential-secrets-psychotherapy-the-inner-child.

2. Bruce D. Perry, "Traumatized Children: How Childhood Trauma Influences Brain Development," American Academy of Experts in Traumatic Stress, https://www.aaets.org/traumatic-stress-library/traumatized-children-how-childhood-trauma-influences-brain-development.

3. "Treating Childhood Trauma," *60 Minutes*, March 11, 2018, https://www.cbsnews.com/news/oprah-winfrey-treating-childhood-trauma/.

4. Lisa J. Smith, "Re-Parent Your Inner Child," DailyOM, https://www.dailyom.com/cgi-bin/courses/courseoverview.cgi?cid=839.

5. Diana Raab, "Deep Secrets and Inner Child Healing," Psychology Today, August 6, 2018, https://www.psychologytoday.com/us/blog/the-empowerment-diary/201808/deep-secrets-and-inner-child-healing.
6. Mary Elizabeth Dean, "Inner Child: What Is It, What Happened to It, and How Can I Fix It?," BetterHelp, updated April 10, 2020, https://www.betterhelp.com/advice/therapy/inner-child-what-is-it-what-happened-to-it-and-how-can-i-fix-it/.
7. https://www.goodreads.com/quotes/1010089-on-writers-workshops-it-is-the-dab-of-grit-that.
8. Serenity Online Therapy: "My Child Within: A Poem to the Wounded Child," http://serenityonlinetherapy.com/my-child-within.htm.

CHAPTER 10

1. Neuroscience News, *Train the Brain to Form Good Habits Through Repetition,* January 28, 2019 https://neurosciencenews.com/repetition-habit-training-10652/.
2. *Indistractable: How to Control Your Attention and Choose Your Life* by Nir Eyal, (Ben Bella, 2019).
3. *Wall Street Journal,* 'Indistractable' Review: Fixing Our Attention, April 21, 2020 https://www.wsj.com/articles/indistractable-review-fixing-our-attention-11570142933.
4. *Wall Street Journal,* 'Phil Hellmuth, 'Poker Brat' by Alexandra Wolfe, Aug. 11, 2017.
5. *Words Can Change Your Brain: 12 Conversational Strategies to Build Trust, Resolve Conflicts, and Increase Intimacy* by Andrew Newberg M.D. & Mark Robert Waldman (Avery, 2012).
6. *A Course in Miracles: Combined Volume* by the Foundation for Inner Peace, (published by The Foundation for Inner Peace 1975).
7. *Mapping Perception to Action in Piano Practice: A Longitudinal DC-EEG Study* by Marc Bangert and Eckart O Altenmüller. Oct 15,2003 https://dash.harvard.edu/bitstream/handle/1/4734539/270043.pdf?sequence=1.
8. *Soft-Wired: How the New Science of Brain Plasticity Can Change your Life* by Michael Merzenich (Parnassus Publishing; 2013).
9. *Power Up Your Brain: The Neuroscience of Enlightenment* by David Perlmutter (Hay House Inc, 2011).

10. *Washington Post*, Harvard neuroscientist: Meditation not only reduces stress, here's how it changes your brain by Brigid Schulte May 26, 2015, https://www.washingtonpost.com/news /inspired-life/wp/2015/05/26/harvard-neuroscientist-meditation -not-only-reduces-stress-it-literally-changes-your-brain/.
11. *Train Your Mind, Change Your Brain: How a New Science Reveals Our Extraordinary Potential to Transform Ourselves* by Sharon Begley (Ballantine Books, 2007).
12. *Altered Traits: Science Reveals How Meditation Changes Your Mind, Brain, and Body* by Daniel Goleman and Richard J. Davidson (Avery, 2017).
13. *Science News,* In pursuit of pleasure, brain learns to hit the repeat button, https://www.sciencedaily.com/releases/2018/03 /180301144210.htm.
14. *The Willpower Instinct: How Self-Control Works, Why It Matters, and What You Can Do to Get More of It* by Kelly McGonigal. (Avery, 2013).
15. *Soft-Wired: How the New Science of Brain Plasticity Can Change your Life* by Michael Merzenich (Parnassus Publishing; 2013).

CHAPTER 11

1. Joseph Jaworski, *The Inner Path of Knowledge Creation* (Berrett-Koehler, 2012).

INDEX

Page numbers followed by *f* refer to figures.